Memoirs of a French Courtesan

Volume 3: Luck

Memoirs of a French Courtesan

Volume 3: Luck

Céleste Mogador

Translated by Kristen Hall-Geisler

Practical Fox, LLC
Portland, Oregon

Copyright ©2025 Kristen Hall-Geisler

Translation by Kristen Hall-Geisler
Original title: *Memoirs de Céleste Mogador*
Translation copyright ©2025 by Practical Fox
All rights reserved

Paperback ISBN 979-8-9903034-2-3
ebook ISBN 979-8-9903034-3-0
Mogador, Céleste
Memoirs of a French Courtesan
Volume 3: Luck

Neither artificial intelligence nor large language models were used to translate, edit, or design this work.

Practical Fox, LLC
Portland, Oregon
www.practicalfox.com

23

Le Havre-de-Grace

THE HEART IS A MYSTERY like no other. I noticed, on arriving at le Havre, that I had a motive for distancing myself from Paris. It was a pretext to write to *him*. A letter postmarked from le Havre and motivated by a voyage would seem less contrived. The first thing that I did when we arrived at the hotel was ask for paper and ink.

> *My dear Robert, the reasons for our separation are so unassailable that you see I've resigned myself to them. Besides, you can't ask a human creature to do more than they're able. I think of you more than ever. Thanks to your care, I've recovered my health. I no longer want to go to the extremes that made me so ill. The sadness that's smothered*

one day will come back stronger the next. I've resumed my friendship with Jean. I'm here for several days, so if you have something to tell me, you can write me here. Think of me.
  Céleste

I had never seen the sea. I could feel how enormous it was in the way it consoled me. My appreciation was mixed with feelings of melancholy. The vastness of the sea made me sad, which distracted me entirely from my grief over Robert. I wondered how people had the courage to entrust their lives to these oversized cradles called ships, which a wave gently lifted one day and swamped the next. To live for entire months between the sky and the water would bring me to my knees.

The hotel where I was staying faced the jetty. On my balcony, I could see far across the sea. As I watched the movement of the waves, it seemed as if the hotel tossed like they did, as if it were a ship. I went back inside and closed my window. It was cold, but the day was beautiful.

Jean came to ask me if I wanted to take a ride along the shore with other travelers.

"Non," I said, wrapping myself in my cape nervously, apprehensively. "I'd rather walk." I took his arm, and we went out.

I bought a bunch of chinoiseries. A blast of wind enveloped me so forcefully that I was nearly lifted like a balloon, along with my purchases. The air that inflated my skirts concerned me a little, but I didn't want to let my little pots go! I walked more quickly than I wanted to. Luckily we were pushed toward the hotel where we were staying.

The weather became so bleak that it was almost dark

as night at ten o'clock in the morning. I got back to the hotel without accident. I tucked away the souvenirs that I'd bought in a drawer. The wind battered the houses, and the panes of glass howled like the furies.

"What weather!" I said to Jean. "It was the right choice not to go out in a boat, since your sea is icy."

"Oui," he said, "it's a real storm! It's beautiful to watch though."

I went to the window and was terrified, but I kind of liked it. Nature's loud voice calmed the passionate voices that growled quietly in our hearts, harmonizing with them.

"You find this beautiful?" I said. "It will make you die of fright! Those poor people who went out in the boat, what are they going to do in their walnut shell against a squall like that?"

"There's no danger. They shouldn't be too far out."

The waves came in like mountains and smashed on the beach. More waves followed, erased the traces of the first, and pulled back with a howl. Farther out, we could see immense masses of water rising with a roar and falling back down over themselves, opening up deep abysses that seemed to plunge to the bottom of the sea.

Sometimes I seemed to be able to distinguish the poor little black dot of a boat. "There it is!" I said. "They're being crushed!"

"Non, non," said Jean. "Those are swells."

"But if one of those giant swells overtakes them, they're done for!"

Forgetting the cold, we opened the window and went onto the balcony. Many people were at the hotel's front door below us, each with a hand to their throat and their eyes unblinking, searching for those who'd gone out.

A man in the crowd despaired and said, "Why did I allow my son to go? They'll be lost at sea!" He wept; he was quite old. His hair was all white, but the old man and his son looked alike. I shared his pain and took even more interest in the boat. I had good vision, so I focused on the distance to do my best to see the boaters.

I saw them first. I was so emotional that when I said to the poor papa, "There they are," I nearly fell from the balcony. I had him come up and stand next to me so he could see better. Someone brought lorgnettes, which didn't do any good. The man's vision was too weak to see anything. I pointed out to him all the movements the boat made.

When I said, "They're moving forward," the poor old man laughed and grasped my hands. When I lost sight of them, he pushed me away as if to blame me, as if I'd prevented them from reaching shore.

"There they are! I see them! They're having trouble, but they're moving."

He pulled me to him, squeezed me in his arms, and said, "Watch, my child, keep watching!"

A hundred times, I thought they were sunk. They were near enough that I saw them roll like a feather, rise, and fall. They were close but still couldn't make it to shore. Two hours went by like this—two hours of agony. At last they made it, pale, defeated, broken by fatigue and emotion.

The old man left my side, running as fast as his legs allowed, to embrace a tall, handsome young man who was about twenty-five years old. I said to myself as I watched the old man go, *He's as ungrateful as a child. He didn't thank me for sharing in his terror.*

But that evening, in the hotel's dining room, he came

to sit next to me. His son thanked me for the interest that I had taken and the service I had done for his father.

I had been mistaken in thinking the man was ungrateful. Instead of one conquest, I had made two. The father wouldn't stop talking about me. He found me charming and adorable, and I was so pretty! I told you that he had poor vision. I had the spirit of an angel! I had only said a few words to him, but I repeated them to him as much as he liked: "There they are! They're safe! Oh my God, I can't see them anymore! No, there they are! They're coming in!"

The son apparently had learned to think like his father. He became more than appreciative, and after two days, he declared flatly that he was madly in love with me.

Jean clearly saw this little meeting, and what was more unusual, he protected this young man by leaving us be. Jean hated Robert. He had sacrificed himself to all my whims to make me forget a single name, a single memory.

My castaway was no great wit. He began to be very annoying. He wrote me such droll notes that I couldn't help but snort laugh. Whenever I ran into him, he always wanted to kidnap me, by land or by sea, either way. He didn't speak of anything less than marrying me, and he was sure, he told me, that his father would forgive him a love that his father himself had kindled. Wasn't I the angel who had saved the boat with my prayers? Could he say no to the woman who had saved the life of his son?

I told Jean that I wanted to dine in my rooms. He asked me why I didn't want to go downstairs, and I said that the father and son were both nuts. They wanted to make me into an angel. They thought about ways to kidnap me, which meant I had to take precautions so as not to expose myself to capture.

"I thought they amused you," said Jean.

"I would never amuse myself at the expense of people who loved me. I don't mean to harm anyone on purpose." I looked at him as I spoke because these words were meant for him. He didn't say a thing.

Jean had a friend in le Havre, and after dinner he asked my permission to go see him for half an hour. He had just left when the door opened. I thought Jean had come back in; I didn't even stop reading. I heard the doorknob of my bedroom turn. I turned around and saw my castaway, more ashen than the day he'd come back from his boat ride.

"Why didn't you come down to dinner?" he said in alarm. "You scared me."

He was very out of sorts. I thought it prudent to speak to him soothingly. I told him I hadn't come down because I had a headache.

"Why didn't you tell me?"

The naïve confidence with which he revealed his little plans to rule over me surprised me so much that it took me a minute to know how to answer.

He went on, "You didn't come down in order to hurt me. You're a tease, like all Parisian women. You love men only to torture them. I love you, and I didn't bargain for this. I saw your passport; you're unmarried. You're going to leave this gentleman and come with me. I'll fight him." He was from the Midi and seemed to have no sense at all.

The conversation had taken a worrying turn. Jean could have come in. He was a cold character, but he loved me and would not step aside for a newcomer as he had done for Robert, who had a previous claim on my heart. I only saw one way out: to tell this young man bad things about myself.

"Look, my friend, think about it. You met a woman who's with a man who is not her father. This shouldn't give you a good opinion of her. Instead of coming to your senses, you set out to love her like a madman, you want to kidnap her, marry her, fight for her. And for who, I ask you? You don't have the slightest idea, so I'm going to tell you: for a girl who ruined her youth, who is not dignified enough to be of interest to anyone, who men take and leave, who could lure you into this infernal life that people only escape after their illusions have been shattered, along with their fortunes and sometimes their honor—in the end, for Mogador!" I thought he'd be repelled by this name.

He said, "Mogador? I don't know what that is, but I love you. It doesn't matter to me what you were, I love you. I don't live in Paris. You can conceal your past at my country estate. Come with me, or I'll follow you wherever you go, even Paris, into this pit that you believe will scare me off. You'll always see me."

"Oh, come on," I said, "be reasonable. Wait a few days. The man I came to le Havre with is going to leave. When I'm alone, we'll see, but I don't want to upset him. He must not find you here. Go, but by God, calm down, and don't do anything foolish until he goes."

He promised me and kissed my hands. He seemed so happy.

Jean came back a few minutes later and said in surprise, "Hold on, you've packed your trunk?"

"Oui. We're leaving tomorrow. Early."

No one was awake in the hotel when I checked out,

leaving my regrets for this poor boy who loved me at least as much as I loved Robert.

24

A Masked Ball at l'Opera— Victorine, Called the Panther

I was only away ten days, but it seemed as if years had fallen away. Jean had taken a holiday with me without my paying any attention to him. I approached my apartment with beating heart. Maybe I had a letter from Robert! The concierge gave me one. I devoured my letter as I went upstairs.

It was long. Robert greeted me in the same way I had taken my leave and lost him. He told me that this was harder for him than for me, that he didn't have anyone to console him. I read this letter many times. He was jealous. A bolt of joy ran from my heart to my head: He was jealous! I had a hold over him. I felt an immense happiness because I had, for the first time, complete awareness of my strength. Love is the ruler of the world, but next to jealousy, it is only a poor, trembling child.

People are afraid nowadays of the rule that certain women have over the nature of their lovers and of the devastation they create in their lives. They demand a miracle, and they look for an explanation in irreconcilable contrasts. On one side, they suppose that women are cruel, hardhearted monsters; on the other, that they are the very embodiment of stupidity and weakness. People are wrong on both counts. The nature of the human heart is explanation enough. When jealousy doesn't kill love, it goads it. It's the whip of the furies, and the soul that has at one time felt its lashes no longer belongs to itself. There are poor women who suffer and die knowing this for a fact. I know too much of the world to not benefit from my experience when it comes to this love that fills my heart.

There's only one way to get him to come crawling back, I told myself: torture him. And, as much as I loved him, I was merciless.

My letters left much to desire as far as style and penmanship, but they were masterpieces of flirtation. I succeeded in all of my wishes. After a week, he was more in love with me than ever. He wrote to me:

My dear child, I'm coming to spend two days in Paris. I'll be at the hotel Chatam. If you could spare an hour for me, you know the pleasure I would have in seeing you.

On Sunday, the boulevard was full of society people. I wanted to move quickly and only succeeded in getting shoved by passersby. When I got to Robert's door, I did my best to seem calm, even cool.

He kissed me and, looking me right in the face, said, "Do you still love me, Céleste?"

"Oui," I said, "but it's better that I get used to no longer seeing you since you are about to marry."

"Non," he said almost happily, "I'm not getting married. I was absolutely on the brink of making a very stupid marriage, but my lucky star rescued me. A serving woman told me things about my fiancée—things that her parents had certainly not told me. Once we were married, it would have been too late."

"This is why you're coming back to me?"

"In part. But more because I love you."

"Really, Robert?"

"Never enough."

We spent a week together. He never left my side. I wrote to poor Jean to avoid them running into each other, and true to his habit of self-denial when faced with the rights of acquisition, he didn't come to see me.

Robert had to return to Berry. "I'll send for you," he said.

I didn't need to ask myself, *Do you want to go?* I spent two months with him.

One day, he received a letter announcing the pending arrival of his relatives. "Go back to Paris for a bit," he said. "As soon as I'm alone again, I'll come get you."

I suspected that this visit hid some new marriage plan and that Robert was only telling me part of the truth. I searched for the letter, and it wasn't hard to find. My intuition had not fooled me: The letter advocated for a proposed alliance that would tie him down, through a of a friend of the family.

I came back to Paris and wrote to him that I was not fooled by what he'd told me. He didn't respond for some time. The poor boy was surely looking to strengthen his resolve. I was less anxious than I had been the first time around.

A hunch told me that all these marriage plans would fall apart. I walked resolutely in the path that I had chosen: I waged a terrible war on Robert's heart through my foolishness and eccentricities. I went to balls, to concerts, to shows. It was the busiest period of my life. My mind at rest had become more reflective, and in this new world, I saw that everything was an object for me to study. After leaving the theater, we went almost every night to supper at the café de Paris. These beautiful salons with golden vases of flowers gleamed in the light. The meal, prepared in advance, was like a feast. The partygoers were young, rich, and elegant. Their names were the best in France, but their lives were meaningless, their characters whimsical and changing. This world didn't at all resemble the one I had been part of while at the Hippodrome.

Léon and his friends, all sons of very honorable bourgeois merchants, were arrogant pedants. They ranted against the nobility, but they were jealous. All those that I knew would have paid in blood for the right to hang a sign on the door of their businesses: "Le Marquis of Such and Such, Tailor. Monsieur le Comte of Such-and-Such, Timber Merchant." They had great fortunes, but they lacked something that kept them from being happy: a little coat of arms to pretty up their papas' invoices.

What pleased me most in my new amphitryons is that almost all of them were somehow connected to Robert. I'd met them at his house. This way, I could be sure he was being kept current on my conduct and that not one of my extravagances was lost on him.

The accident is the most skillful of mechanisms. It arranges very curious combinations. In the whirlwind where I was newly thrown, I made new acquaintances every day. In this life, friends and lovers disappeared like shadows, and then you ended up running into them again without saying hello.

I was attached to a woman older than me. There was in her character something like my own present disposition, an analog that made me study her attentively. Two years earlier or later, had she crossed my path, I probably wouldn't have cared. But at this precise date, she exercised a kind of influence over me.

She was no great beauty, yet she was one of the most fashionable women. She was rich and regarded the courtesan life she'd renounced with contempt. Maybe she had been lucky and it was out of spite that she'd been rendered nasty, which happened all the time. She always tore her dear friends apart in the best way, with so much verve that only their bones remained. She said, "I leave them behind because they are spoiled."

This Panther, so ferocious to everyone, had taken a great affection for me. I have no idea why.

One night, I wanted to bring her to l'Opera.

"Non," she said to me. "I won't go."

"Why?"

"Because smart people don't go there, or if they do go, they put on a disguise."

"They'll take it off for you. Come—you'll make me very happy."

"I'll do it to make you happy. I don't ask for more than that. But five years ago I gave my black taffeta domino mask to a poor girl to wear to her mother's grave."

"We'll rent one."

"Let's go, then. I'll let myself to do this. We'll dine beforehand. If I run into old friends, I do not want them to say the Panther has been defanged. A glass of champagne, a mask—and beware to all who fall to my fangs."

After supper, I looked at her with a certain anxiety. Her eyes were shining. If she'd only drunk one glass, that would have been fine! Under the vestibule at l'Opera, she stopped a man in a cape who was following several other masked men.

She said to him, "Not so fast, Gerbier. Say goodnight to your friends. This is the second time that you've pretended not to see someone in full daylight at the Hippodrome. I forgave you this lack of acknowledgement once, and I believe you said that you were in a bad mood. Did you decide to take on this stag hunt as a personality?"

The gentleman, who was about fifty and stammered a little, told her to shut up, that he wasn't alone.

"Oh, monsieur is with family today. Forced to leave his little room, he came to the Opera ball to shape his heart and mind."

The gentleman plunged into the crowd to get away from her.

I asked, "Who is that?"

"An idiot! At his age, he's grooming an actress. I hate actresses in general, and that one in particular."

"Why?"

"Because she's no good!"

"Not good how, as an actress or as a woman?"

"She's bad at both. Talent, for most of these women, is in the details. Theater doesn't enrich them; it ruins them. They can't retire without subsidies from strangers.

What is the stage, with few rare exceptions, but a display window?"

"Not all are like that—"

"Oh, of course not," she said, laughing. "I'm leaving out the old women. And maybe one in a hundred among the young. But the rest live on the backs of European luxury. Those women you saw passing through made a lot of money in London, Vienna, and St. Petersburg. They're always on the road. It's an export business. Besides, it's a tradition within the family. She'll be like her mother, who lost her daughter to this life. Someone should set them all straight."

We'd come to the door of the foyer.

"Hello, beautiful mask," said a man who was leaving as he hugged my waist.

"You know that gentleman?"

"Non," I said, freeing myself.

"That's good. I'm going to give you his name and everything you need to know about him: He's the grand commander of the Order of Rats. Well," she said to him, "is your servant still well behaved?"

"Why would you ask me that?" said the gentleman, trying to place her.

"You told him last year, on new year's day, 'Francis, I give you this old boot! If you serve me well, you'll have the other next year.' Does he finally have the pair?" Everyone laughed.

We went into box twenty-one. I was surprised to find people already there. I thought that Jean, who had given it to me, had invited some friends. Victorine spoke to me without disguising her voice.

A woman in a domino turned around. I saw her eyes shining through the mask, then I heard her say into the ear of a gentleman, "The horror! There is a snake here. Who opened this box to these women?"

"I don't know," said the gentleman, "but I'm going to send them off."

"Oui, oui," said the lady, lowering her hood.

Victorine and I heard it all. The orchestra had been making noise, so she'd spoken loudly enough to be heard by the gentleman.

He got up and said, "Mesdames, this box is taken."

"Oui," I said, "but it's taken by me. It is mine."

"Surely you're mistaken."

"Non, call the usher. I gave her my ticket."

He did call her. He was wrong. Their box was next to mine. We were right, and they had to leave. During these explanations, Victorine watched the lady attentively, and unluckily for the woman in the mask, Victorine recognized her.

When she got up to leave, Victorine blocked her exit and, taking her measure, said, "It is her! I'm a snake? Fine. You'll hear me hiss."

The lady in the mask said not a word but left and reentered the box to our right.

When she was seated, Victorine said to me, "Do you want me to tell you why they call me the Snake? The story will amuse you and our neighbors too."

There were many from society in the box to our left. Not a word of this little scene had been lost. They could see this was going to be serious, and they settled in to listen. The lady in the mask turned toward us and looked at Victorine defiantly.

"Imagine," Victorine said to me, "I was loved by one of the most fashionable men in Paris. He loved me very much, but he traveled in high-society circles. A woman of high birth was chasing after him. She knew of our liaison, and she threw a fit. She endlessly asked him what charm a girl like me could have, a courtesan—elegant, it's true. But even in all my luxury, I should inspire disgust and scorn, because it could only be like the story of *One Thousand and One Nights*. I had great power over my lover. He told me of these lovely conversations, saying, 'If you want, I won't go to her house anymore. She's crazy about me, but I'd sacrifice her for you.' So he no longer went to see her. She waited hours at the door of the club. He ended up being touched by her humility. She raised herself above me. I would have wanted him less if she hadn't been an honest woman and if she'd had the indulgence of anyone else. But she was too sly to be interesting. The guiltiest people are our sworn enemies, and we do them harm. This one came down well below me. My lover returned to me, but she wanted him back. This annoyed me. I found letters from her at his house. I had asked her to back off, and she did no such thing. I got my revenge. I took her letters and sent them to her husband after having made the addressee's name illegible. Before sending them on, I read these letters; they were very funny. She told him, 'Don't hold back! Treat me like a whore.' That's the way the world goes! We demand to be respected, while these ladies demand to be treated like shit. Down here, you see, Céleste, half of the people steal from the other half. I cried thief. That's why she calls me a snake."

The woman in the mask was not prepared for this level of sniping. While Victorine was speaking, the unlucky woman didn't dare leave. It was easy to read her emotions in the trembling of her fan. Her companion made a face that I'll remember all my life. The young men in the next box laughed.

After a few seconds, the lady complained of being hot, left, and didn't return. The moment the door of the box closed, the Panther tossed out her name to finish off the insult. I chastised her for saying the name so loudly.

"Why? Because she had a husband and children? If she doesn't respect them, why should I respect them? I know the stories of many others. Their chambermaids talk more than me."

"Come one, let's take a turn around the foyer."

I took her out to look for the person I was waiting for. She stopped before a young man leaning his back against a column.

"Bonsoir, de J…. How is your father?"

"You know me?" said the startled young man.

"Apparently, since I asked for news of your family."

"Fine, my father is doing better."

"I understand why you seem so depressed. The money will grow. Poor boy, go!" She began to laugh. I asked her why the money was going to increase.

"It's going to increase for him. For some time, he was trying to borrow from a lender I know. He wanted to tender bills of exchange, but the lender didn't want to accept them.

"'You're wrong,' the man said. 'My father is sixty years old!'

"'I thought he was much younger,' said the lender.

"'Fine,' replied the young man, 'but he's sick and he won't last long, I'm sure. Thus you'll be paying at the date of maturity.' The business was not concluded. If the father got better, he had to pay more."

"This is a sordid gentleman, your young man. He writes off the life of his father too happily."

"It's true, but there are many like him."

"That's awful!"

"I don't disagree," said Victorine. "It's a little the father's fault. They raise them badly. While small, the children are fed by strangers. Later, they eat with their governesses. Then they're sent off to school outside the family, which they leave at seventeen or eighteen. Romantic love overtakes them before they have even dreamed of loving their parents. They rack up debts, and their fathers don't pay them. The best of them wait for their father's end; the worst of them wish for it. If I had a child, I would raise him at my side, and I would not make him spend ten years of his life learning such things that should bore young men, since as soon as they're free, they'll go to hell to forget them. Oh, you see," she said to a man who crossed our path, "you annoyed your wife, who sent you to l'Opera."

"What are you trying to say?" said the gentleman, who seemed angry.

"There, there," said the Panther, "don't get carried away. You know that you started out like that, but you had your reasons. You told yourself, 'The horns, they're like teeth, it hurts when they break through. When they've come in, they're for eating.' You are a living example of this, since by the grace of your wife, you have a place that keeps you alive."

The gentleman frowned. I held on to Victorine, who I trailed into the crowd.

An hour had passed, and I still didn't see Jean. This began to worry me. My companion picked up on my thoughts.

"Why didn't he come?" she asked.

"I have no idea. He sent me the box I asked for,

but I suppose he's sulking. If Robert knew that, he'd be enchanted."

"Your Robert will adore you," Victorine said. "You're taking the only way. They say that we're monsters, but whose fault is that? Be sweet and good, and they'll come to you. I seem to recall being sweet and good for a long time. My first lover, who was a raider, made me sleep on the tile floor in January, but he kept me warm! When he left, I felt the cold, and I did as he did: I left. I got back at my first lover with my second, the second with the third, and so on. I was called the Panther, the Snake, but I was loved. Now I'm hated, I live alone, and I bore myself. I hoard disgust. I never have a good thought for anyone; I no longer know how to say anything nice. I hate happy people. I got back at those who created me by taking away my youth and my illusions. I'm thirty—that's young for an upstanding woman, but I'm old. No one speaks of me anymore without saying 'the old Victorine,' which damns me. It's the punishment I deserve. If I'm being honest, I feel like my heart didn't age. I only suffer from being abandoned."

"It's your own fault. Why didn't you hold on to your friends instead of making them hate you? Everyone is afraid of you."

"Friends! Law-abiding people don't have any, so how do you expect me to have any? I don't give away enough money."

"Oh, my dear, you are hopeless. Let's go."

After taking her home, I went into my house, depressed. I fell asleep under the influence of this awful genie who, while disparaging everyone, boasted of not having any more illusions.

That's how women lose themselves even among

themselves: After the degradation of the body comes the degradation of the soul, the worst of all degradations.

25

Vive la Réforme!

When I woke up the next day, I went to see Frisette. She was glad to be alive rather than dwelling in darkness like Victorine.

There were a lot of people on the street murmuring among themselves. I stood near a few clusters of people and listened in without understanding a word anyone was saying. When I got to her place, I asked Frisette what was going on. She didn't know either.

"Do you want to come out with me?" I said. "Maybe we can learn something."

"I'd love to! Let's go."

Once we reached the boulevard, the crowd there was even larger. Lots of people were laughing, so we smiled too. We could hear, in the midst of the noise, the word *reform*!

I stopped a young man and asked him what this meant. He answered with an air of importance, "We want reform."

"Aha. And what kind of reform?"

He looked at me, shrugged, and walked off without answering.

"Did I say something wrong?" I said to Frisette, who laughed.

"Lady, don't know you what reform is?"

"Oh, like you know?"

"Non!"

We found ourselves on the boulevard Bonne-Nouvelle, in front of the café de France. Lots of young people were on the corner. Some of them recognized us when they saw us and shouted, "Long live Mogador! Long live Frisette! Long live reform and pretty women!"

The curious and the flâneurs pressed around us. We were desperate to escape the masses that surrounded us. The color drained from my face. The insult glided in on a whistle; the air was charged with menace. I had the feeling that something extraordinary was about to happen.

I went into the house at no. 5. I knew Mme. Embargé there, whom I'd asked permission to visit, though there had been fewer people outside at the time. She opened a window for us and we saw the dark and shining pool of blue that they call "the people." It moved and grew like a storm! It reminded me of Lyon. I was scared! Then, as everyone went to eat dinner at six—even those who wanted to start a war—the street cleared.

"Go," said Mme. Embargé. "There will be a riot tonight. Go home."

"Come dine with me," Frisette said to me. "What else would you do, eat alone at your place?"

I accepted. It was ten o'clock when I took my leave. I walked along the faubourg Montmartre and the boulevards. Coming to the rue Lepelletier, I heard an explosion. The crowd reacted with a long shout. They were running away from the Bastille. I waited before continuing on.

"Where are you headed?" asked a man in his forties.

"Monsieur, I wanted to go home, place de la Madeleine."

"Then take another route. You can't get through this way. There's been shooting in front of the ministry of foreign affairs." With that, he disappeared.

I kept moving forward, but with trepidation. All of the faces were marked by terror; each regarded the other with distrust. I took the rue Basse-du-Rempart. It was empty. I walked along in silence. I thought of Robert. *A revolution!* I said to myself. *A revolution that ruins people, that forces the nobles into hiding. In times like this, you see the kinds of people who take huge bribes. What if Robert needs me, needs my life!*

This thought struck my heart like a bolt of lightning. I remembered that in Lyon, the rebels who plotted the revolution, and I was ashamed of my egotism.

I reached the corner of the rue Caumartin. The pharmacy had been converted to an emergency room where the poor wounded were receiving treatment. At the sight of blood, my heart became overwhelmed by charity.

I felt tears in my eyes. Crying! It's all women can do! Because they don't understand how they work, they can't do anything about these huge, infernal machines they call wars and revolutions.

Once I had gotten home, I wrote to Robert about everything I had seen, telling him for the first time ever: "Don't come."

I couldn't sleep. The whole building was on alert.

At four in the morning, someone knocked on the carriage house door. The concierge was afraid, so before opening up, he asked, "Who's there?"

I was listening at my window. "Open up! Open up!" I called to the concierge. Him, him, at such a time. "Oh, Robert! Why did you come to Paris? I was so relieved to know you were in Berry!"

"I could go back if I'm imposing on you."

"Imposing on me! It's fine. It's a happy thought that I hadn't let myself have. I thought of your safety before the happiness of having you near me. It's unbelievable, non?"

"Non, my dear child. I don't know what is happening! I was leaving yesterday for Chateauroux. When I got to the station, I couldn't find a carriage to take me. I hoisted my travel bag onto my shoulder, and here I am."

The day after he arrived, he went to rejoin the first legion of the national guard. This made me mad with worry. The post at Madeleine had burned! They had left powder and charges in the post, which had exploded in a chain reaction.

Robert came back at five, blackened by dust and drained by fatigue. He had helped defend the barricades.

A loud noise could be heard below my windows, so I went to look. About a hundred well-dressed men were discussing some questions, doubtless something raised by the events of the day. In the end "oui, oui" won out, and everyone made their way to the carriage station to set fire to the little wooden guard's shed. It was the carriage drivers who lived in the quarter having some fun, just like in Lyon. Down there, it was a tax to be paid.

I asked Robert to leave—and to take me with him!

He promised he would as soon as we could get out, because he was needed at home. We left the next day. I began to breathe again when we reached Étampes.

I didn't dare speak to him of his marriage proposals. He was the one who told me that he'd been rejected—he was free! I was beyond happy.

Robert, young and handsome, with his name and his wealth, should have succeeded at everything. He should have succeeded in finding a good match, given all the imbeciles out there who had none of these advantages. But Robert had a fault that was a constant hurdle in his life: he didn't have the slightest sense of moderation. As soon as he wanted something, he no longer wanted it. I believed it was a great strength of character when I was at his house; I was wrong. This was violence. He didn't know how to master his passion nor his desire. He would regret the next day what he had done the day before. I often suffered for it. I saw perfectly well that he picked fights. He loved me, and I bore the brunt of his volatility. I couldn't approach him, and he scolded me for being obliged to come see me. And yet, through my affection for him, I was transformed. I lived at his side with the greatest refinement in taste. I gave him advice that he didn't listen to—because it was good advice.

His need was huge. The chateau that he kept was dilapidated. Only one single room showcased it former splendor. Everything was three hundred years old. It all needed repairs, chateau and grounds. The farmers, already in debt, didn't pay the estate rent, and the people Robert owed money to became less forgiving. I remember that Robert borrowed sixty thousand francs at 20 percent over collateral. We were in the middle of a revolution; cash, which was all being sold at this price, was hard to come by. Robert had a good heart, and the Belgian farmers came to the house to ask if they could return to their country. Berry is an unhealthy place; there are fevers that don't break, and the work there is punishing. The plowmen are slow because they're undernourished. It was only because of the weight of poverty that they'd come here. Many sold their wheat and ate potatoes or chestnuts themselves. The Belgians couldn't adjust to this kind of poverty. They had been taken care of by Robert's father, who had hoped to plow half of his extensive lands despite their being thought barren.

Robert consented to their departure. He even gave them some money because they were very upset. One had lost his crop to a hailstorm; another had seen three of his family die; the others were sick. The best lands remained untouched.

Robert wanted to make his own fortune. He didn't listen, or he wasn't happy. But this cost him dearly.

Chateauroux isn't a real place; it's a kind of faubourg that you walk across in search of a town. The inhabitants are rude; many push this rudeness to the point of savagery. When the uncultured nature of the rural man rose up, he became ferocious. There were horrible crimes in the town squares. Many chateaux had been invaded; the caretaker of one of these chateaux had been sliced by a scythe. The chateau de Ville-Dieu was half burned down inside; all that remained were the stones. The area where we lived was calm, however, and they liked Robert. I struggled not to worry about him.

Once I was leaving Chateauroux in one of his carriages when I heard the shouts of masses of children. There was a carriage in front of me. The driver turned his head and said to me, "We can't get through. Look, they're attacking the carriage of Mme. de … with stones."

My blood turned to ice. I went back inside and begged Robert not to go out anymore, or if he did, to remove his coat of arms from the carriage.

He took this very badly and told me that they could kill him if they wanted, but that he certainly would not remove the coat of arms. That would be cowardice. I didn't sleep all night.

I was afraid that my sojourn to the chateau would affect the high esteem they had for him out here in the country. One day I saw about forty men armed with loaded pistols on the grounds. They arranged themselves near the chateau. I heard their shouts, and I saw them from my window as they became more agitated and brandished their weapons.

Robert was playing billiards with Martin. I went into the room crying, "Save yourselves! Hide, or your lives will be lost!"

"What are you talking about?" Robert asked as he clasped me to hold me up. I was so pale, I was shaking so hard, that I was about to fall over.

"What am I talking about? I'm saying that there's not a moment to lose, or you'll be assassinated. There are shouting armed men down there. Now can you hear them? Save yourself. Go into the cellar, and for the love of God, don't wait a second longer."

Convinced that he would follow me, I saved myself and headed for the side stairs that led to the cellar. It was as if I could see the barrels of their guns, could hear the shots. The basement of the chateau was enormous. I walked along the dim, damp cellars, my knees buckling at every step. I turned around and saw, with a feeling of unspeakable terror for Robert, that he hadn't followed me. I listened, but I didn't hear anything. I was beneath a beam of light coming in through a basement window.

"Oui! Oui!" shouted the voices. "There! Let's put it there! It's the best. Take the pickaxes… Look out! Look out!"

"Non! Non!" answered other voices. "He's going to die, he's too grand!"

Too grand! To die! It rang in my ears.

What are they talking about? I asked myself. *Too grand! Robert! They're plotting his death. My God! Why didn't he listen to me? I must see him.*

I walked in the shadows, following along the walls.

All of a sudden, shots rang out. My heart stopped. I let myself slide to the floor.

A meager thing, the courage of a woman! I wanted to keep going, but at each new shot, I felt myself falter. I wanted to fade into the walls. Everything I loved in the world was upstairs. I'd have to climb the staircase. The barrage of gunshots continued, but it seemed to slow down. I reached the upstairs like a charging horse.

"Where did you come from?" Robert asked as he lit a cigar.

"Where did I come from? I came from the cellar, where I hid and wept for you—for no reason, it seems, since you're laughing. What was going on, this little war that had me so frightened?"

"Listen, you'll figure it out."

I did, and I could distinguish the words, "Long live monsieur le comte! Long live the republic! Long live the trees of freedom!"

We went onto the terrace. A man came up to us, doffed his cap, and said to Robert, "It doesn't bother you, sir, that we'll plant a tree in the name of freedom? If it bothers you, that's okay. It's a fun story, and I'll drink a cup to your health."

"Non, it doesn't bother me," said Robert, "since I gave it to you, along with a quart of wine. As long as you don't plant it in my garden, it's all the same to me."

I finally understood. The thing that was too grand and going to die was the poplar tree. They all made fun of me, and it was hilarious for a few days.

I received a letter from my maid. I had debts and bills to pay. If I were a man and in business, I would have been the most careful of accountants. The thought of a late payment set me on edge.

Robert, despite having so much wealth tied up in land, was more broke than me. I could not and would not ask him for help.

I told him that I needed to go to Paris, set my affairs in order, and pay my rent.

He opened his desk, rummaged in its cubbies, and said, "My poor Céleste, I want to give you what you need, but I can't. I have nothing. I'm going to borrow two hundred francs for your trip."

26

Roulette

Back in Paris, I was very embarrassed. I had some jewelry that Robert had given me, and getting rid of it seemed impossible. The republic hadn't made anyone rich. All my friends, men and women both, were broke like me.

I found myself dining wh Lagie and Frisette.

"Come gaming," they said. "There are a lot of gambling houses now. We play roulette every night. There are a lot of people there, but the best is on rue de l'Arcade."

"But," I said to Lagie, "it's dangerous there. The police haven't approved gambling houses."

"Non, but there's nothing to fear. They don't let just anyone in; they take precautions. Come on, we'll introduce you."

I had a hundred francs to my name and a whole lot

of boredom. I decided to go, despite my fear of the police.

When we arrived on the rue de l'Arcade, our carriage stopped in front of a huge, beautiful house. It was all so calm that I thought Lagie must be mistaken.

"It's not possible there's a casino in here," I said.

"Come on, come on," she said as she tugged on my dress, "but don't talk so loud."

We went up a staircase painted red and lit by oil lamps. I stopped, gasped, and asked if this hellfire was going to make itself at home in heaven.

"As close as it can get," said Lagie.

We went up to the fifth floor. She knocked, and a bell rang three times. A servant came to open the door. Her answering the door seemed clairvoyant. This would have dumbfounded some less sophisticated people, but it made me laugh. This was the job of well-kept servants like this, like Robert's.

From the entryway we went into a salon. We were welcomed by a woman in her thirties who had once been very pretty, and she still was, if only her pale, thin face were not engulfed by a forest of black curly hair in long ringlets. It made her seem wild. Sometimes she looked like a devil, sometimes like a ghost. She offered us seats near the fireplace, then said to me, "You've never been here before, mademoiselle. I've never had the pleasure of seeing you."

"Non, madame, this is the first time."

"Ah! Are you lucky at the red and black?"

"I don't know, madame. I rarely win at cards."

"I hope that you'll be luckier here." She got up to chat with other people.

"Who is this woman who's hoping I win?"

"That's the mistress of the house. She says that to

everyone, but you know she doesn't mean a word of it. When I say that this is the mistress of the house, I mean that the lease is in her name. The man who keeps the bank is a kind of amphibious beast; no one knows where he comes from, what country. He speaks several languages, and he has a lot of money. To keep from getting arrested, he put the house in her name. If the police come, they'll take her away."

The allure of gold must be powerful, I said to myself, for this woman to be resigned to being arrested and maybe sentenced to prison. I watched her, and kept an eye out for her taste in luxury, which would drive her to poverty. But her outfit was simple. Her black silk dress had been altered several times, and everything about her seemed depressing. I didn't understand. Each time there was a knock on the door, she flinched in her chair. Her eyes were glued on the door with anxiety. When whoever it was entered, she regained the words or the smile that had been frozen by fear.

"Why don't we begin?" said a tall young man.

"The banker hasn't arrived," answered the mistress of the house as she checked the time. He couldn't be late. The clock chimed eleven.

"Are you in a hurry to lose your money, Brésival?" said a fat, common-looking girl who was called Pouron. She swatted the young man familiarly.

He was distinguished. His face was nice enough, but too pale. He pushed her away playfully, but he seemed to be impatiently waiting.

I was near Lagie, so I asked her what was going on with this man they called Brésival.

"Oh, you like him, right?" Lagie said, looking at me. "He doesn't have anything at all to do with women; he loves gambling too much for that. He's married, and he has children sweet enough to eat, but he'll end up gambling away their layette. He spends every night here and loses everything. He works himself into a lather over everyone, and then he throws a fit. You'll see it if he loses before the morning."

A moment later, a gentleman appeared. His arrival was accompanied by a general gasp in the room.

"At last! All is not lost! We were about to leave. You're late."

"Oui," said this man who'd entered using a key rather than being let in, "I'm coming from a party. I present to you a night of new games and good times."

"All right, then!"

The new arrival seemed to be about forty. He wore a black suit and white tie, and his complexion was bronzed, his hair brown. He seemed like he might be Italian. He spoke to the mistress of the house to give her instructions and chide her. He noticed me and regarded me for a while, which pinned me in place.

The maid opened a double door, and I saw a huge well-lit room with a long table covered in green cloth, a roulette wheel in the middle, and chairs all around. Everyone went in, but I stayed near the fireplace in the first room.

"You're not going to play?" asked the mistress of the house, who remained in the room to receive late guests.

"Non," I said, "I'm not in the habit of gambling, and I'm afraid of not being able to protect my money. Besides, I'm feeling uneasy. Aren't you afraid?"

"Oh, sure!" she said. "But I can't let him see it. I'm running a great risk."

"You make a lot of money though?"

"Moi!" she said, laughing sadly. "The only thing I have to eat is regret."

"Then you love this man who came in late, since you're keeping the house for him?"

"Me! Love him!" she said as she leaned toward me. "I hate him. I consider him beneath me, but I'm afraid of him."

Someone knocked, and our conversation ended. Now I really wanted to know more about these strange characters. People came to smoke in the salon where I was. As it was impossible to keep chatting with her, I got up to play.

The mistress of the house, whom they called Pépine, passed close to me and said sweetly, "Don't you know how to play? Put your hand on that old man's down there. He has good luck at gambling."

She moved on to offer cakes and refreshments to the players. She stopped by the person she'd mentioned and looked at me as if to say, "This one." I had a louis in my purse, and I put it on red near his money.

The croupier called out, "Place your bets, gentlemen! Nothing ventured, nothing gained!"

He turned a crank that everyone watched with anticipation. Myself, I watched with curiosity. I'd never seen it before.

"Black loses, red wins!" the croupier said, then he used his little rake to collect the money. Soon he said again, "Place your bets, gentlemen! Red or black!"

"Are you playing?" Lagie asked me so loudly that everyone looked at me.

"Oui, but not for long. I only have five louis."

"And the ten that you just won. That makes fifteen,"

said the decorated gentleman. "You've passed twice—and hold on, red takes it again. You have twenty louis now. Leave them?"

I swear to you I wanted to snatch them up, but they called me a chicken, so I left them. I was overcome by emotion, the game slowed down, and I had to get out. At last they said, "No more!"

I turned to look and saw nothing. My poor twenty louis were absorbed by the black. I met Pépine's eyes. She gave me a small smile and let the red curtain in the doorway fall. She seemed like a hallucination, a devil. What else would you see in a house like that? Was it possible to think of anything but hell? Fine! It's awful of me to say, but I prayed to Satan to win back my forty louis, and when I heard, "Black loses, red wins!" I jumped and knocked into two people. They began to see me as a big gambler. The banker gave me a smile that he intended to be charming, but it was more of a grimace because I was jingling his coins.

I went into another salon to count my winnings.

"Go back in," Pépine whispered to me. "Always bet, but risk nothing…"

I went back to the game.

"Did you pull a Charlemagne?" Lagie said when I returned. "Win big, then leave?"

"Moi! Non. I was overly excited, so I went to get a glass of water."

I took a chair and sat at the table, which I hadn't done before. Mlle. Pouron made it easy to be lucky, because I kept winning. I had a little shy of two thousand francs in front of me, in gold, which was very rare at the time. They paid one louis and ten sous for change. I was so happy that I wasn't tired. The candles began to sputter, and everyone was tired, beat. The women's lipstick had smeared. The men who had lost, and therefore weren't speaking while they hoped to win it all back, could no longer maintain their composure. They let their tempers show. I didn't dare take my leave, which I very much wanted to do. The women, jealous of my streak, pushed me to place a huge bet. I made them die of rage that night, because I went on to win four thousand francs.

I cringed when I saw a man search his pocket, hold out his empty hand, and look at everyone. The more the gamblers liked gambling, the more they were down. It was a fever, a delirium, like madness. Despite my lack of sympathy for people who didn't know how to overcome this passion, I pitied him. He seemed to suffer deeply. I asked him if he wanted a few of my louis, that maybe they'd win for him. He quickly snatched up what I offered and lost it all in five minutes. He looked at me again in case I was going to give him more money.

Just then Pépine, who was serving chocolate, stepped on my foot. I hadn't looked at M. Brésival, who was still making eyes at the gold in front of me. No matter how much he gambled and lost, it was nothing. But when he no longer had enough on him to keep playing, he became furious. That's just what happened. He punched the table, which only made a muffled sound. You couldn't hear the clink of the coins because of the cloth covering. He upended the roulette wheel as if he wanted to smash it. All the women surrounded him. He was cognizant, that's the word, that he had been robbed, by hook or by crook, and he wanted his money. I escaped to the first salon, clutching my money, which I had no intention of giving up. Besides, I hadn't won it from him.

La Pépine was watching the scene serenely. I tapped

her on the shoulder and said, "Thank you for the advice. I must go."

"You're done? Okay. Wait a little; you can't go out alone at this hour. Where are you living?"

"Place de la Madeleine, no. 19. Come see me—I'd like that."

I escaped by giving six francs to the maid who let me out. I was only truly sure that my money was mine when I was far away from that house.

Back at my place, I tallied my fortune. Never had anything come along just when it was needed like this. I thought of Robert, of the fact that I could go back to him without being his dependent, of the shopping that I was going to do to return to his side. I fell asleep after spending a hundred thousand francs on my dreams.

The next day, I spent the day running to my usual merchants and tossing money their way. At this time, this was not a common thing to do. I was welcomed with open arms. Those who serve us and then get rich off our weaknesses cover us in kisses, in compliments. Deep down, they can't stand us; they detest us. It's very simple: We are their living. I have the same level of affection for them that they have for me. I pay them regularly because the idea of owing them anything is anathema to me. I borrow from them when I need credit, knowing they'll charge me double. But I need to buy things, so I don't say anything.

Back then, though it's not that long ago, it wasn't like now. Actresses and kept women could only get credit at a few select shops. If I went to the Ville de Paris to buy a dress and said, "Send that to me, *Mademoiselle Céleste, horseback rider*," they would not hand over the package without touching cold, hard cash.

Today, all the big houses—including the Ville de Paris, la Chausée d'Antin, les Trois Quartiers, le Siege de Corinthe—deliver to your house. If they bring your goods while you're out, they leave them and don't charge for the postage for six months. And they'll sell it to you for the same price as they would anyone else.

That's those who would have our business. Everyone pushes us to these ridiculous depths, which can ruin so many of us. Lots of people take advantage of the benefits without any of the responsibility. The merchants use all the temptations. If I weren't held back by my conscience, I would have amassed three hundred thousand francs in debt: the cashmere shops, the jewelry, the carriages, the furniture—all offered with no limits.

I resisted because I thought of the future. I said to myself, *It'll have to be paid for. Some women don't have the backbone, so they make mistakes and end up losing everything.*

I went around to all my creditors by myself in 1848, the year of the revolution!

I bought myself some dresses, undergarments, and above all a travel case in silver, which I'd wanted very badly. Robert's friends had them, and I wanted to be like the fashionable people. I was trying very hard, but the only thing I had in common with them was my travel case.

At least Robert loved me. If there were clouds in his love, those clouds were made small in contrast to his real troubles with his apparent fortune. I was happy with this love.

My gambling winnings had changed my thinking. I only thought of winning again, to have lots of money when he came back.

27

La Pépine

THREE DAYS HAD GONE BY since my evening at the rue de l'Arcade. I struggled between the desire to go back and the wisdom to not. The fear of being arrested in this den of loss stopped me, while the siren of winning drew me in.

I was lazing about at eight in the morning when, in the middle of my musing, my nosy maid Marie came in and announced that a lady wanted to speak to me. I didn't have a foyer at this apartment, so I said, "Have her come in."

Hold on, I said to myself when I saw my visitor.

"Am I disturbing you?" said Pépine as she sat near my bed.

"Not at all. I was just thinking of you—that is, of your house. I won a lot the other night."

"I know," said la Pépine. "Why haven't you come back?"

Great, I thought. *She came looking for me so that I could pay back what I won. I'm going to make sure she can't repossess her money.* "My word," I said, "I wouldn't go back there for anything. All I have left of that fortune is five hundred francs."

"That's too much. Never bring that to my place. You only need to lose a hundred francs, and if you do, you won't ever have to play again."

I looked at her. I had been wrong—she wasn't here to get the banker's money back. "Would you like to have breakfast with me?"

"Oui," she said, "only don't let anyone else in. No one needs to see me at your place. This must seem odd to you that I'm here, though you invited me. I passed by your door, and remembered that you liked me. You aren't at all like the women who are usually around, who take their pleasure in causing me pain."

I understood her to be saying that she was jealous because the banker had mistresses among the gamblers.

"They hurt you? Why do you put up with it?"

"Because there's nothing else I can do."

And I saw in her black eyes, which flashed like lightning, that it required a huge amount of strength to rein in her anger.

I had a very lovely dining room furnished in carved chestnut pieces, with panes of colored glass in the windows. It looked like a cabaret in there. We sat at the table.

I was afraid of this woman—not afraid that she would do me wrong, but afraid of her way of being. I was always on the defensive as I watched her. She was nothing but friendly toward me, and I forced myself to be less wary. We made small talk.

"How thin you are!" she said as she displayed her own neck. "This life is going to kill me! Spending every night there! Quaking every time someone knocks! Even those stronger than me wouldn't last long."

"Then why do you do what you do? It must be truly exhausting."

"I don't have a choice."

"How is that possible? You're forced to work til you're ill?"

"Oui."

"By the banker?"

"Oui."

"Aha! He's the devil, then?"

"Something like that," she said. "But the devil only offers bliss. This guy offers suffering."

"What are you going to do?"

La Pépine's Story

I knew him in Italy, my home country. He lived under a false name with a woman who was still beautiful, even at her age. I was eighteen at the time, and I was pretty. He pursued me tirelessly. I lived alone with my mother, and we ran a business together. He hardly left his house. I often saw him with this other lady, but he told me he didn't love her. Finally I let myself fall for him, and we became lovers.

One day, this woman found me at his house with him and said, "You poor little thing. You're done for. Do you know what this man is? He's a captain of industry; he bows to no one. I was a young widow, so he was with me not because he loved me, but because I was rich. He ruined me, tortured me. I no longer have anything to my name. He has to support me. There's probably shame behind his pretend love for you. Your youth alone isn't enough. Watch yourself: He'll sell you if you don't have anything of worth."

What she said made me sick.

"Adieu," she said. "This is the last straw. I'm left without any defenses. I went to him without courage, and I'm paying for my weakness. Let my example be a lesson. Watch yourself!"

She exited slowly, and I followed her automatically toward the door. A voice inside my head told me to do as she said, to listen. My lover blocked my way and protested so much, made such promises, that he convinced me that she still loved him. It was only jealousy that made her say such things. I believed him.

This was total bullshit. A few days later, I found him again at this woman's house, even though she'd said goodbye to him in front of me.

"You see," he said to me, "I can't stop."

That night, he sent word that he absolutely must speak to me. When my mother was in bed, I went out.

"Listen," he said, "we can't live like this anymore. I don't have any money. If I did, I'd give it to you. If someone could loan it to me, we could leave town together."

The idea of breaking up with him made my stomach turn. I searched my mind for some way to hold on to him.

"Or," he said, "if I had money, I would give it to this woman to get rid of her."

"My God," I said to him, "if I had money, I would loan it to you. But we don't keep any money at the house. My mother sends the week's income to her accountant because two women on their own can't keep anything valuable on the premises. Sometimes the sales are rather large."

"Oh!" he said, in a way that should have warned me to be on my guard. "Oh! Your mother does a lot of business. You're useful to her, you're the one who makes it all work, you keep the books. You're the signatory."

"Oui."

"Then I'm sorry to have broken up with you." He kissed me and cried. "I couldn't get any word from my parents for a month. It's impossible to live with this woman another month! If you would…but you don't love me enough… Besides, what would they say about you? You don't believe in me."

"Oui," I said, "oui, I believe in you."

"Wonderful! Go get some money in your mother's name. They'll give it to you. I'll take it, and you'll report it being stolen. No one will know a thing."

When I didn't answer, he threw himself at my feet to beg my forgiveness for what he was about to say: "My love for you makes me crazy. Do you want me? Forgive me…I'll leave tomorrow…"

"Non," I said, "I don't want you to go. But I don't dare do it. If it were a small sum…but I think you need a lot."

"Oui," he said, inhaling. "At least ten thousand francs. I know, I'll go, my dear Pépine. Come see me for the last time tomorrow."

I returned to my room feeling terrible. I couldn't sleep all night. My mother called to me late in the morning; she was worried.

I went to see my lover at noon. His trunks were packed. The thought of losing him made me insane—oui, insane. I told him to wait one more day.

My mother was not yet up. Knowing that some days

she didn't get out of bed, I thought she wouldn't know what I was planning to do. With the devil on my shoulder urging me on, I arrived at my mother's banker. I said that she had an important purchase to make and asked the teller to give her two thousand francs. It was so typical for me to come ask for funds, sometimes even larger amounts than this, that he didn't bat an eye.

He said to me, "Would your mother like a receipt?"

"I'll leave a note. That should be enough."

"For the boss, that's enough," said the teller, "but he's not here. I have to follow the rules."

"How long is the boss out?" I asked nervously.

"A week."

I went back home. My mother was very ill. I went to my lover's house to tell him of my defeat. I began to cry again, and I became even sorrier. I told him to wait until the next day, that I was going to try to win over my mother.

"Take good care of yourself," he said. "We could lose everything. You sign the same name as your mother; just put down *widow* instead of *daughter*. I'll take the money from you before she even misses it."

The devil held on, no matter how I fought. In the end, I promised my lover the money that evening. I went up to my poor mother's room and asked for her signature to authorize a note that someone had presented downstairs.

"Who?" she asked me.

I said some random name and added, "Don't write 'to authorize,' only sign it. If he only gives me one payment…"

Poor Mother! Her trust in me was so great that she signed without asking me any more questions. I ran to my lover's house to ask him if there was anything else to do.

"Non," he said. "Fill out the page: 'I request that you give my daughter, who brings you this note, the sum of twenty thousand francs.'"

"Twenty thousand francs!" I cried out and stopped writing. "They'll never give me that much."

"Fine! Write *twelve*, but it has to be twelve."

I wrote.

I was back in about an hour with my money, which he took from me before I could hand it over to him.

"Take care of everything," I said. "I'm going back to my place, since my mother could ask for me. Until tomorrow!"

As I was leaving, I found the other woman I had seen a few days before at his door. She stopped me and said, "Listen to me, poor child! You're jealous of me. That's the method he's using to get rid of you. He tells you that I love him and you believe him because here I am at his door. He's lying to you, and you're fooling yourself. I want him to hand over some jewelry of mine that he has so that I can sell it to pay for my trip. I stopped at the place I'm staying while I wait for this asshole to make good on what I own. I know that he has the money, but my presence allows him to rile you up. Keep your guard up, my child. Keep your guard up!"

I didn't sleep for several days, I was so worried. My mother got better. He didn't say anything about taking my money; he always pretended to be waiting on news from Paris. My mother told me that she'd be able to go downstairs the next day. I lost my mind. I went to find my lover, all in tears, and told him that I couldn't go back to her without money.

He thought a second, looked at me, and said, "I'm going to bring you with me to Paris. We'll come back when I have what I need."

I consented to go with him, though he already seemed not to love me anymore.

Thus follow the ten years where my life has been attached to his. He makes me do all the work. I sacrificed myself to make sure he was safe, yet he makes me want to kill him. I can't live like this anymore.

"Why don't you leave?" I asked. "Turn him in?"

"Do I have a choice? When I arrived in Paris, I didn't know a word of French. Where could I have gone? It's hard to live in this huge city! Turn him in? Aren't I as guilty as he is? Besides, I was scared. He left me for a week or ten days at a time without even wondering if I had anything to eat. My lack of money never crossed his mind. This house brings in a lot of money for him. He was less interested in me. I had more freedom, and if my plan succeeds, I won't be here much longer."

"Does he steal while gambling?"

"He's capable of it," she said almost in a whisper, "though I don't know for sure. He's mysterious. He has people who win a lot in his entourage at all times, and they hole up with him the next day. The old man who I pointed out to you the other day is one of his followers. He brings that same crowd around often, and he wins a lot. If you only knew how much I hated him, this man who is no longer mine and who makes me the most miserable and humiliated woman! All the girls that he takes as mistresses insult me and talk shit about me. I'll get back at them when I get back at him."

"Why don't you just leave him?"

"I've got nothing," she said. "But in a little while..." She clammed up. I could tell she didn't want to share her plans with me, so I didn't ask any more.

We finished lunch and went into my room.

"Listen," she said, "you cried to me the first day I saw you. I've told you my business, so you can see that I trust you. Would you do me a favor?"

"With all my heart, if I can."

"You'll be able to."

"Say it, then."

"When I escape from this man's house, I want to bring my things with me. Would you let me bring them here, little by little? I don't know anyone but his friends, and I'm going to hide from them. You won't say anything, will you?"

I promised.

"Come tonight," she said. "Whatever you do, don't say that you've seen me. Don't speak to me too much. I'll tell you who to associate with at the table."

"Thank you!" I said. "I'll go tonight for the last time. I don't like the risk, but you can count on me."

When she had left, I thought about all she had told me. If I didn't want to get the money so I could go back to Robert, I certainly would not have set foot in that terrifying house. Even the friendship of the mistress of the house wasn't reassuring.

⁙

I arrived at midnight. There were more people from fashionable circles this time than the first time I was there. The game was animated. I watched this man whose story I'd heard that afternoon. His face conveyed his character. He disgusted me.

It was strange how easily vices overcame all barriers to sate these passions.

Cash was in such short supply at the time that the government synchronized paydays and nationalized workshops. The landlords demanded a third of the rent, which was worth fifty francs, but the pawnbroker wouldn't loan out any more than a hundred francs in those days, and business was in agony. But there were mountains of gold, silver, and bills on the table. The gold was worth fifty francs to the thousand in exchange. The emigration of the population during the Revolution made everything more expensive by the day.

Where in the world did he get this money? At what trouble and at what price should he have it? The gold changed places, leaving to the losers only a muffled sound on the double-thick fabric.

The old beauties of Franscati were there, though they found it depressing compared to what they'd seen. One of them, called Blais, saw that I was happy to win a thousand francs and said to me, "Why do you celebrate such a small win, my dear? I had a thousand francs in front of me, I had a carriage, gorgeous diamonds. I don't remember showing as much joy in those as you for these louis. How far women have fallen."

She was trying to say I was a cretin, and since the lesson was delivered loudly, I answered likewise.

"You'd do well to hold on to something of your splendor. I hope that when I'm your age, though I might have less than you, that this will serve me well. You should tuck away some of those riches that you invested so badly."

In reality, this woman—who I'm told was once

so beautiful and lived life to the fullest—now lived in depressing poverty. She had a son in the navy. This poor child loved her, and he sent her the little money he earned. This was her main source of income.

I exchanged looks with Pépine, who told me to play conservatively. I had already won three thousand francs. I wanted to leave, and I even got ready to go and put my money in my purse. Then a knock on the door made everyone jump.

"That's not the signal," said the croupier, who was a terrified shade of pale.

A second, louder knock sounded.

"It's the police!" all the gamblers said at the same time.

I felt like I'd died. La Pépine was next to me, white and shaking.

"Let them in!" said the master of the house to a servant. As he did, he released a spring. The table opened in the middle, and all the money disappeared into a hidden compartment.

The sound of surprised laughter pulled us from our terrified stupor. It was a group of young men who'd forgotten there was a signal to get in. They laughed at the scare they'd given everyone, but I couldn't calm down. My teeth were chattering. I went into the other room and found la Pépine alone.

"Do you understand," she said to me, "what I put up with here?"

"Oui," I said, "I'm leaving and never coming back. Get out as fast as you can. You know where I live. Adieu."

I thanked God that night in bed for my having been scared enough to leave.

28

Deceptions

THE NEXT DAY, I WAS walking along the boulevards when someone walked up behind me, touched my arm, and said, "At last, it's you. I've found you."

I closed my eyes. I didn't recognize the voice. I was frightened.

"Don't you recognize me?"

I opened my eyes and saw...the drowned man from le Havre, who I thought I'd left forever on the shore.

"Where have you been hiding yourself?" he asked. "I've been in Paris for a few months. I'm no longer a country boy. I've learned the real name of the angel I found between two storms. You didn't fool me. You're called Mogador. People told me only the worst about you, but I don't care. I love you more for it. We have an account to settle together. Do you know that you left me stranded? Anyway, where do you live?"

I said to myself, *Great! It's always the same. He's headed straight for the goal. Does he imagine I'll ask him in?* I didn't want to give him my address, but he wouldn't leave me alone. But I had to go home, and he followed me. When I reached my door, I said to him, "Au revoir."

"What, au revoir! Do you think I'll just leave? Fat lot of thanks! I've been looking for you for a month, and when I find you, you don't give me even five minutes to rest at your place. In Provence, where I'm from, we're friendlier than that."

I started to laugh. I went up the stairs, and he followed. Once we reached my apartment, we chatted for quite a while. His proclamations of love were unbelievable. It was getting on five o'clock, and I was to dine at a friend's. I asked him to let me dress for dinner.

He left, but at ten the next morning, he was back at my place. I was afraid that in order to shake him, I was going to have to leave Paris. I told him all my faults, and he set them like diamonds in his dreams, surrounding them with flowers but not wanting to look at them. I brought him around little by little to the idea of just being my friend. Every day I told him I loved another man and that I was too blunt to lie to him. He gave in and no longer told me how much he loved me. He was devoted to me in a way no one would be to a woman who isn't theirs.

One day, while I was feeling down, he asked me why. I bared my soul to him and made him see the dark side of my life. He left without saying anything.

The next day, he returned in triumph.

"You think, Céleste, that friendship is not possible

between men and women. Fine! I've found a way to show you that it is. Yesterday I wrote to the prefect to ask for your record to be cleared, to have you taken off the rolls as a courtesan. You'll be free. You owe me your freedom. Now do you trust in my affection?"

A bolt of joy rose from my heart to my face. Then, considering all the obstacles, I reconsidered.

"You doubt I can do it?" he said. "You'll see. I'll have a response in six days. I'll only come back to see you once I have it."

I thanked him from the bottom of my heart, but I had a feeling nothing would come of it.

I received a nice letter from Robert, which helped me be patient, because the days were starting to seem like one horror after another. I only had ten more days to wait to see him again when a messenger brought me a trunk and a little box.

"Mlle. Pépine asks that you keep these until she comes to get them," the messenger said.

I didn't dare say no; I'd promised. However, at this moment, when I was being so careful, seeing this woman and storing her things seemed reckless. What was in the trunk? Maybe something that would get me into trouble. I looked for a way to get myself out of this but couldn't find any reasonable solution. So I waited until the next day.

I was about to write her when a carriage stopped at my door. I saw la Pépine enter the building. She was dressed in black and held her veil over her face like someone in hiding.

"Ah!" I said as I opened the door. "I was about to write to you. I can't keep these trunks here without knowing what's in them."

"It doesn't matter. I've come to fetch them," she said. "I'm leaving France this very night. I'll take them with me. I'll take back what he stole from me. I'm headed for my country. Tomorrow his casino will shut down, and he'll be arrested. He won't be able to come after me. I'm very happy. It's been ten years that I've waited to get my revenge. Now it's done. Adieu, my dear friend, and thank you. I might never see you again. Trust me: Don't go into gambling dens anymore. You can't tell the cheaters from the honest people."

She hugged me and had Marie take her trunks downstairs. I breathed more easily when I heard her carriage pull away.

A week passed without news about the request that had been made on my behalf. Then I received a long letter from my drowned man. I took it that the response was bad, since he didn't bring it himself. I read:

My dear Céleste,
I am too hurt by my failure to come to you myself. I tried yesterday, but alas!

They asked me who I was to you. I said that I was your friend.

"Do you have the intention of taking her with you, to emigrate, or to support her to ensure an honest life for her?"

I promise you, my poor friend, that I was embarrassed, because you haven't wanted to come with me. And my wealth is entangled with my father's, so I could not promise to provide you with an alternative income.

I left there very upset, my dear Céleste. Trust that if I could have done it, I would not hesitate, no matter the sacrifice I had to make. But I have my father, and I don't dare ask him for anything. I walked out of there desperate. Forgive my foolish hope that I gave you. If I could show you how much I love you, you would see that I was sincere.

I had to laugh out of pity for myself. I had been lured in by this silly dream. I had put my life on hold all week. Why so much dreaming? What did I do for him? What was he to me? He had written a request, that's just great! You don't even have to dictate it; a scribe composes one for you for a franc. He loves me. Wonderful. That made me happy, since I wanted him to feel bad. I detested him for the memories he'd brought up, and the hope.

Individual justice is not the strong suit of well-bred people, and even less for the ignorant poor who envy everything. The lies seem unjust, and they resent feeling truly bad for their wishes because they don't know how to reason. Women are of course annoyed by being treated like queens one day and slaves the next. They pity themselves and accuse men of weakness, of unfairness. The heart closes itself off to pull away from lovers who are embarrassing. The women become envious, mean to the point of hatred, on the day that they're forced to hate themselves. As life went on, I could count myself among those women. I saw things as they were, and I called it as I saw it. Women like me are not appreciated, but the women in my life are so unpleasant that I would rather have enemies than friends.

29

The June Rebellion

SUMMER ARRIVED, BUT IT WAS sad, for me at least. When you're down, the sun seems wan. Robert returned to Paris at last. Then everything seemed beautiful and joyous to me, despite the sinister rumblings that could be heard everywhere. The alarmists, who talked about unrest a year before unrest existed and a year after there was no more unrest, had a great time. The paving stones seemed to raise up to let you see the huge cannons ready to reveal their troops. Minds were the black powder, newspapers the fuse. Finally it became clear that they were going to fight again: Civil war, the monster that had scared me so, was going to open its gaping maw. God alone knew the blood and the victims it would require to sate its hunger.

The general panic was at its peak: What was going to

become of us? Robert was very worried; he couldn't pay his rights of succession, and he couldn't touch the farmer's tithes. He had come to Paris to try to settle his debts.

The June rebellion went off like a bomb, and the terror grew extreme. A boutique in my building was converted to a post for soldiers of the mobile guard, and Robert rejoined the national guard. I was on the porte cochere with my neighbors, collecting news. Our quarter was calm; the streets were too wide to be barricaded. We heard a deep rumbling.

A detachment from the line of small mobile units had been disarmed and run from their post. They were boiling with rage. They wanted to go into battle. It was almost impossible to calm them down; they were only held back by promising them action the next day. They listened with us. They told us what they had seen, what they knew. In a time like this, we made quick friends, and they were given food and drink. I can't think of them now without my heart breaking. Poor children! They were twenty; the oldest were maybe twenty-one. They played at being soldiers, a sad game that cost nearly half of them their lives. They were radiant when they were taken away and led into the fire.

One of them returned the next day to see his mother. He had a band on his arm because his brother and ten of his comrades had been killed. Then he went back to the battle.

Le Marais was under siege. Entire households had been put under the blade of the sword. They had shot through windows. I felt something strange shake loose inside me.

"Are you coming from Saint-Louis?" I asked.

"Oui, but I couldn't stay there. It's the center of the

rebellion, and the houses are like Swiss cheese."

I let out a loud cry. My mother lived in Marais, rue Saint-Louis. My tenderness toward her returned along with my fears.

"Marie," I said to my maid, "quick, get me a shawl and a hat. I have to see my mother right away. My God! If something's happened to her... My intuition tells me I'll arrive too late. Hurry, Marie! Hurry!"

"Where do you want to go, then?" the soldier asked me. "You can't get through anywhere. There are rules posted, and the artillery is bivouacked on the boulevards. No bourgeois goes out. You won't get twenty steps."

"I'll say that I want to see my mother. They'll let me pass."

"I assure you they will not, unless you have a pass from a commissioner."

"Fine, I'll get one."

"Madame, I am begging you, don't go out there," Marie said to me in tears. "You're going to get yourself killed. Bring me with you."

"Non, my girl. Stay. The worry is worse than death. My life, beautiful business that it is! Is Robert not risking his? Where is he? After I have seen my mother, I'll look for him."

And I left.

The commissioner's office had been transferred to the minister. They barred my passage to see him twenty times, but I begged, I insisted, and I at last came before him. He recognized me from the Hippodrome, where he had been a regular.

"What do you want, my child?" he said to me kindly, which reassured me a little.

"Monsieur, I came to beg you to give me a pass to go

to rue Saint-Louis, in Marais."

"But that's impossible. There's no way in, and they're fighting there. You will not get there."

"Oh, oui, monsieur, I will get there if you give me a pass. My mother lives there. Her house is one of the ones that's been fired on this morning. The battle's been taken up again on the faubourg Saint-Antoine side. I'll get there. I beg you, give me a pass. I'll bring it back to you in ten hours." Tears fell from my eyes. I couldn't hold them back.

There were two gentlemen in his office who wore embroidered ribbons on their lapels. "She is brave," said one of them, "you have to hand it to her. She's worried about her mother. It's only natural."

"Hold on," the commissioner said to me as he handed me a paper. "Be careful, and don't take the side streets."

"Thank you! A million times thank you, monsieur!"

Outside I found Marie, who had followed me.

"Go on then," I said. "I don't want you to risk your life."

"Non. I don't want to go. I'll follow you no matter what you say."

I didn't have time to discuss it. I left the neighborhood. I was constantly told to go back the way I had come. I showed my paper, and they looked at me in surprise, but they let me pass. We reached the place de la Bourse, where groups of men in dove gray led others dressed just like them: These were prisoners who had been disarmed. That was the only difference between the groups of men.

After a thousand detours, I came to the rue Vendome. The street was guarded by mobile units. They were black with gunpowder, and the whole street was still warm from the fires that had been set.

"Open the shutters and close the windows!" they yelled as they looked up, right where we were going. "They shot from behind those shutters, and from their hiding spots they picked us off like flies."

The first battle had worked them up, because they seemed antsy. They were waving their guns around heedlessly, a danger to themselves.

I passed near two soldiers who were not of the same opinion. They were arguing.

"Wait, look, there's only one way to reach an agreement," said one. "Put twenty-five paces between us. We'll each pull the trigger on our guns. Whoever drops the other is right." As the other man set out to walk away, my blood turned to ice.

A shot rang out. Everyone jumped on their weapons and laid down cheek by jowl, not knowing if the attack came from among themselves. It was frightening to watch.

I took refuge in the corner of a porte cochere, and Marie pressed herself against the wall next to me.

Seeing that it was a false alarm, they put down their guns. A second shot fired in our direction. I saw the flash of light leave the barrel, and then I heard the whoosh of the bullet and the sound of it embedding itself in the wood of the door I was leaning against. Marie made as if to duck, but I held her up while looking above us. The bullet had lodged itself two feet above our heads.

"Let's go. Get ahold of yourself and come on, Marie. Why did you follow me if you're such a chicken?"

"Oh, madame, I'm not a chicken, but I am scared."

She was shaking all over, which made me laugh, if one's allowed to laugh at a time like that.

The gunfire never stopped. They were shooting cannons in the faubourg Saint-Antoine.

The windowpanes that had been shattered by bullets both the day before and that very morning fell like rain. It felt as if the earth trembled under my feet. I saw the house where my mother lived, which gave me courage. We had to go up the stairs of a high barricade across rue Saint-Louis, all the way to rue des Filles-du-Calvaire. We were escorted over with care, since they shot at soldiers who came from our side of the barricade. We were brought to the entrance of my mother's house. It was half demolished, and the concierge had been killed the day before. His wife and three small children stood around his bed.

"Where is my mother?" I said to her without any consideration of the fact that I was disturbing her in her grief.

"Who is your mother?" the crying woman asked brusquely. She had no idea who I was.

"I'm sorry, madame, I'm asking—"

I hadn't finished my sentence when Vincent came in.

"Hold on!" he said. "It's you, Céleste. Your mother is upstairs. Go up! She's doing well. Thank God, it didn't hit us. At least it got warmer here."

His face and his voice reignited my hatred for him and my indifference toward my mother. I passed him to go out.

"You're not going up?" he asked me.

"Non, I learned what I came to learn. Adieu."

He called after me. I left without responding.

"Well, my poor Marie, she's living for everyone except me. Robert, if I only knew where Robert is! Come on, Marie, we're going to try to get through via the boulevards. They should be less dangerous than the side streets."

However, we had to take streets up to the rue du Temple; it was the only way they'd let us through. At this point, I saw a lot of people I knew. They were surprised to see me and helped me pass. The boutiques were closed, except for one or two every so often that were serving as medic stations. The sides of the boulevard served as camps for the soldiers. The roundabout was covered in hay for the horses, cannon parts, ammunition, stockpiles of arms—they lacked nothing. Some wounded who had been bandaged by medics were among the men, listening. They could no longer fight, but they could hear. I thought that, at a time like this, everyone would be depressed, ashen with emotion. But their faces were calm. This bravery was sublime to witness.

The battle came near, and their turn was about to come. They seemed happy, without fear of death, as if they had no weaknesses.

I walked on, stunned by what I'd seen. What a magnificent sight! Something to ennoble one's soul. Why aren't I a man? It would be beautiful to see these regiments face the enemy. I seriously considered all that I'd seen as I walked and was proud of being from the same country as these brave people.

"Non, I'm not mistaken," said a young man in a medic's uniform who barred my passage. "It's Céleste! What are you doing, my dear friend, out here with us?"

I recognized him as Adolphe's friend. I grasped his hands and kissed him without asking, glad to have the chance to tell at least one of these men how I loved and admired them all.

"I came to find news of my mother. Do you still see

Adolphe? How is he?"

"You haven't seen him, even though you came from that direction? He was sent up to the Bastille. I was told this morning that there were wounded doctors and he was one of them."

I became pale as death. I was dumbstruck.

"Come now, don't take it so hard. If I'd known it would have such an effect on you, I wouldn't have told you. Besides, we don't know for certain. You have a pass, go to his house. He lives on rue Bourgogne."

I clasped his hand without answering and took off so quickly that the crowd parted to let me through. The idea that this man was wounded, maybe in danger of dying, made me very worried.

At the place de la Concorde, they refused to let me cross the bridge. The cavalry was bivouacked there. In the center were many men dressed in black and wearing the same ribbon on their lapel that I'd seen at the commissioner's office where I got the pass. I went up to them and addressed myself to the oldest of them.

"Monsieur, could you give me permission to pass over the bridge? I would like to go to rue Bourgogne."

"Certainly, madame. If you'll take my arm, I'll escort you across."

I declined, in his best interest. What would people think if they saw a representative of the people give his arm to Mogador? He insisted; I resisted. Another joined him, and despite my wishes, I was accompanied by both of them. I thanked them as best I could and, as they left, wished them the best possible luck. All along the docks on the other side of the bridge there were national guardsmen. As I passed through the middle of the crowd, I heard such hearty laughter that I turned around. It was

M. Charles de la Gui…, a friend of Robert's.

"Oh, she is powerful!" he said to me, laughing loudly. "There's a gentleman in my company who said, as he saw you coming across, that you're going to have to be arrested because you're probably a card-carrying rebel. How's it going? Where are you going? Need me for anything? It's such a pleasure to see female face."

My story about my escorts made him laugh like a child, and then I moved on.

"Remember me to Robert if you see him," he called.

I heard him, but I was too far away to answer.

Once I reached rue Bourgogne, I stopped at Adolphe's door as if I were afraid. The concierge came to me.

"Who are you looking for, madame?"

"M. Adolphe, please."

"This is the right place, but he's not here. He was wounded in the leg, so he's at his mother's."

"Do you know if his injury is serious?"

"It's hardly anything, luckily."

I left my name with him and went on, not reassured, but less worried. My thoughts returned to Robert.

He was waiting for me at my place. He let out a huge cry of joy on seeing me. His worry did me good. He looked me over and seemed happy to see me. Robert, he's my family! He's all I have in the world. Forget the rest. When he was near me, I could ask nothing more from heaven. This love was forbidden for him, and by all rights of elite society he should have left me. But the republic gave everyone something else to think about. Robert felt less put upon and gave himself over to me without holding back. Two songs were being sung constantly at the time: "To die for the fatherland" and "The people are our brothers" (at this line, everyone would raise a fist, then put our hands on our hearts) "and the tyrants are our enemies!" I don't know if Robert had political opinions. Probably, but as he had infinite wisdom, he never spoke of it, especially to me. He said that women who occupied themselves that way should be beaten. That was my opinion too; we agreed on this point. But once when a singer came into our courtyard, he pelted him with two-sous coins until he left. I called him a bad brother of mankind and a bad citizen, which made him laugh. It was very innocent.

Robert was waiting on money before he could leave town again. I offered him what remained of my winnings. He refused and waited a few more days.

Paris was in mourning. Many people had died, and hope was far from returning.

Robert went to his business agent's. When he came back, he told me, "Still no money! But I need to leave; I need my estate. Listen, Céleste, I love you very much, but I'm not rich enough to keep you along with all these responsibilities. If you want, my chateau is unoccupied. Bring your furniture; you won't have to pay rent. We'll live happily at my place, and I'll make the necessary changes. If someday we break up and I marry, I will pay back what I owe you."

That was one of the best days of my life.

I went to the owner to tell him I was moving out and that he should try to rent my apartment for the price I was paying. I went to the post office to send my packages. All that took a few hours.

I had a considerable number of furnishings; it couldn't all be shipped without paying an enormous freight bill. I asked Robert if I shouldn't rent a small space for the bedroom furniture, which we could make a pied-à-terre in Paris, in case we needed it. He approved of this idea. I took to the streets and the next day found no. 42 rue de Londres, a small vacant apartment for six hundred francs. There was one bedroom, a salon up front, a little dining room, and a kitchen at the rear. I rented it that day. I had my furniture brought there for a Persian room, and I put the chestnut dining room furniture in the salon.

Everything was ready for our departure. I forced Robert to take five hundred francs in gold that I had. At the time it was almost a fortune. The same day, he brought me jewelry worth more than three thousand francs. I scolded him, but he wouldn't listen. I should have been content not to contradict him. However, I found this expense foolish, and I wished he hadn't. He paid a lot to make himself feel able to accept my five hundred francs.

30

CHATEAU LIFE

WHEN WE ARRIVED AT THE chateau, I pulled out my needlework and began to work.

My trip to Robert's wasn't as precarious this time. I foresaw that he would extend it. Since I was moving from a bustling city life to a more tranquil existence, I needed something to do that would help me pass the long hours of solitude that, though we were almost royal, were no less lonely. I dressed modestly. I didn't want the country people to have any reason to call me lazy or say that I would ruin Robert.

When it came to everything else, I'd set myself an impossible task. The luxurious life bored me, and I abhorred being still. So everyone who crossed our grounds to get to one road or another saw me at the window of my room, doing needlework without a break.

The women who had made the tapestries in the house said that this would become an obsession that would make me forget to eat and drink. I was at work by eight o'clock every morning, and I stayed at it until nightfall. I had brought along Marie, who was my rock. I never went out, and poor little children came to see me. Then I put down the tapestry, and using the Persian curtains and some old fabric found in the chateau's armoires, we improvised a sewing atelier. My little girls left with good dresses.

Little by little, the people of the house came around to me. The daughter of the house manager came to see me. She was twenty-three; in my world, she would have been terribly ugly, yet she was very virtuous and tolerant. I liked her a lot, and I thought she liked me too.

This life seemed to me to be for the privileged. Every day I had a little more freedom. Sometimes I went horseback riding. If I was down sometimes, it was because I was afraid of having to leave this life that fulfilled all my wishes. I dreamed of ways to assure myself that it was mine. Robert loved children; if I had one, maybe he would love me even more.

One little girl came to see me more often than the others. Her name was Solange, and she was lovely as an angel. She was my favorite. Her parents were quite poor, and they had seven children. I gave all that I could to my little Solange.

One day she said to me, "Why don't you come see me, demoiselle? My little brothers would love you. Grandmama is blind, but she's not deaf yet. When I bring the sweets that you give me, she hears that just fine. I'll give you milk from my goats. It's not far from here, le Ris. When will you come?"

"I don't know, but I'll go one of these days with Célina, the daughter of the manager."

"Oui, good," said the little girl as she jumped with joy. "That day, I'll put on my nice dress that you gave me, and I'll put up Grandmama's hair in a chignon, because it's always undone."

I'd read the books of Mme. Sand, and I made a party of visiting the landscapes she'd described. I went to see Mare-au-Diable. What a crock! I found a small pond like a vase full of ducks. My idea of the country as being enchanted was disillusioned.

Everyone had the fever. Everyone was weak and thin. Even regular faces became rare, and the soul was heavy. You would think it the depths of some wild country, civilization had slowed down so much. The country people were sick, and their little cottages fueled the misery. When you go among them, it's awful to see. They live more meagerly than savages. No one can care for themselves, and none worry about the health and vitality of their parents. This seventy-six-year-old man who lived near us fell ill. They didn't want to call for a doctor because that would cost money. They day I learned of this, the doctor happened to be at the chateau. I asked him to call on this poor old man.

He came back soon enough after having seen the deathly ill man. "Well," he said to the daughter who was with the old man, "I've been sent too late. There's nothing to be done."

Do you know how she responded? "Oh, M. *Doctur*, it's shame that I *ain't* known that *this* morning."

"Why?" asked the doctor.

"Because I would've bought the nails for my father's casket."

"That's no problem," said the old man to his daughter. "You'll find them on the mantle in a little pot."

You have no idea of this kind of savagery. They would let you just die! They all have a field, acreage, a plot; the unluckiest have a little more. This man shortened his life to work for what he had, and they would let him die rather than touch him.

The little money that Robert gave me served as charity funds. I couldn't watch this misery without my heart breaking. No one who saw them in their houses could be less struck by it.

So, on Sunday, when the bagpipes went by, everyone went outside. The girls wore white caps and silk shawls; the lads, as they were called, had a traditional shirt, sometimes a jacket, and a big black felt hat with a wide brim. They paired up and followed the music to the clearing where they danced. Then the ruckus began. From noon to six o'clock, they didn't stop. By the end, the only thing you could see was a cloud of dust. The next day, the spot would be marked by a huge square made by the dancers.

The men, who'd been sober all week, drank wine on Sunday. The first glass went straight to their heads, and they kept on going. It was impossible to make them understand that a little every day would do them good and give them the strength to work. They didn't care, and drank, if they were able, four liters on Sunday. They forgot about mass. The pastor constantly pleaded with them and came to Robert to make his case. But there was nothing Robert could do about it.

I don't know if they loved me in the country at the time, but I'm sure they didn't hate me. My moving into the chateau did Robert no harm. Once I paid for musicians, since Robert allowed dancing on the grounds. It was a huge party, and I was invited. I danced the bourrée. They gave me points for being steady on my feet.

The head groundskeeper had three daughters. Once was named Justine, a small, brown-haired thirteen-year-old. She was always with me. She was charming, well-behaved, and a hard worker. I showed her how to do needlework. I dressed her, and she was wise as an adult, and very attached to me, I think. In the evening we all played badminton.

The gardener had two daughters, and one of them often came along with us. She was sixteen and as strong and as tall as me. Everyone thought she looked like me. No one ever saw her sister because she was epileptic. They kept her out of sight with someone always at her side. They said she was a rare beauty. One day, I went into her room, and though I had been warned, I was surprised by the vision before my eyes. I saw a scrumptious creature sitting in an easy chair near the fire. She didn't move. When I spoke to her, she moved her lips, rolled her eyes anxiously, and didn't answer. Her sister rushed in from outside.

"Oh! So sorry, madame, she won't respond. She's mute, and she's giving us trouble. When her attacks overcome her, she gives us a sign to put her in bed. We don't dare leave her, as we live in fear that she could start a fire. In our homeland, Burgundy, the doctors refused to help her. The merciful God would do better to call her home, because she suffers every moment. Yesterday, we closed all the doors because we were afraid the count would hear her. She was shrieking loudly. Luckily we're far enough away from the chateau. She'd been calm for several days. It's just that she's so strong, when she thrashes about during these episodes, we can't bring them to an end. She hits herself. She'll end up killing herself. It's so hard to watch."

I could not pull my eyes from this face. Despite what had just been said, she was calm and unmoving. Her gaze followed our lips. She was beautiful even as she languished. Her skin was translucent, her lips red, her teeth small and white, her features impeccably even, so that she looked like a porcelain doll. I said some words to her, and she looked at her sister as if the one had life enough for both. I left with tears in my eyes, asking myself how God had created something so perfect if he wouldn't give her a soul and clarity of mind.

※

Winter was coming on. Robert was happy at the thought, since soon he'd go hunting with the dogs. Apart from some small lovers' quarrels, the time passed quickly. However, I was often anxious at the thought of the future. I could see moments of melancholy pass through Robert's thoughts, but he didn't say anything. His friends from Paris came to see him, and he squared himself up to welcome them. He made it, but this cost him a lot of money. His generosity went beyond anything you could imagine. He didn't know how to do anything halfway.

One day Robert said to us during dinner, "If you want, tomorrow morning, we'll go hunt deer in the fields. Céleste will be in the party."

Everyone was enchanted by the idea—Montji above all. He was one of our oldest acquaintances. He's the painter who made the portrait of Lise and later one of me. Robert knew him through me and said to him during the revolution, "The arts are going to suffer. Would you like to come stay at my house in the country?" Monji had accepted. He also accepted with good humor the invitation to the hunting party, though it was dangerous. He didn't hold a horse as well as he did a paintbrush.

At five the next morning, everyone was ready. The horses were saddled and impatient in the courtyard. Montji, who had never tried to even mount a horse before he came to the chateau, didn't have anything to wear. Robert had to lend him boots, jacket, and breeches. All of it was a size too big. His helmet fell over his eyes. He mounted a little mare named Henriette, who, without being mean, was skittish. As soon as she began to trot, Montji had us dying laughing. When he gripped her with his legs, she bucked. When he released them, he lost his seat and slid toward her mane.

He of course wanted to stay at the back of the party, but Henriette did not share his opinion. She had been trained by the keeper, so she didn't want to be away from the dogs. Poor Montji was always at the front, despite himself, bouncing two feet out of his saddle. He was brave, but I was really scared for him. He lost his balance with every bounce. He didn't know the bridle from the reins. I had placed both in his hands, and out of the fear of not knowing which to use, he hadn't let go of either.

When we came to the end of the path through the grounds, we came to a huge open area, unfarmed land that belonged to Robert. In other countries, this might be called a moor. It was magnificent hunting ground. It stretched out, unbroken, like a wide road. Apart from some low bushes, you could follow a deer or fox in plain sight. The keeper unleashed twenty hounds, who came to hunt together and explore each clump of briars. La Tembel, an attack dog who was digging around a little, gave a bark. Everyone rallied around her, and a large deer bounded in front of her nose and past the legs of our horses.

The non-clairvoyant Montji let out a whoop of joy. Henriette, seeing the dogs point, took off like an arrow. Montji let go of the bridle to straighten himself in the saddle. Henriette took advantage of this freedom. Poor Montji took her mane in one hand, the saddle behind him in the other, and thus abandoned himself to mademoiselle Henriette's literally unbridled passion for the hunt. I followed them closely. He jumped the shrubs and dams like the wind. Luckily for him, the deer was gone. The dogs lost their voices and they came back to us, so Henriette stopped. Nothing bad had happened to Montji, but he shivered like a plum tree. Robert and Martin laughed good-naturedly, and I did too—once my fear passed.

Montji was in the middle of settling himself when the dogs picked up a new trail and took off again. Henriette took up the chase with them, while the unlucky Montji was mounted on her neck, practically at her ears.

As soon as he could, he set foot to earth. Henriette's punishment was to hear the hunt without being able to follow it. She kept her nose and ears turned toward the dogs. It was impossible to lose the hunt with her, even in the forest, as long as you let her go where she wanted.

After being strung along, the dogs finally took their deer, who'd been exhausted stiff by the run. We rallied the dogs, who pranced all around us because there were lots of spoils to be had. Montji remounted Henriette, who had calmed down, and walked back to the house. We made it back by eleven o'clock. Lunch was delightful, at Montji's expense. He grimaced as he took his seat.

Forest hunts are also nice. I think that knowing how to ride a horse helps. We would hunt wild boar in the forest of Chateauroux, six miles from our chateau. The keeper, his dogs, and his relay horses left the day before to sleep near the meeting place. The groundskeeper would get up at three in the morning to scout the woods with his dog. For our part, we had to get up at four. Robert would shave and put on his white velvet breeches, soft boots, chamois jacket, blue riding coat with lined sleeves and velvet collar, gold belt, ivory-handled knife, black velvet cap, and hunting horn to complete the costume. It fit him perfectly. The white cravat was de rigueur. Once on the hunt, he paid little attention to me; he was all for St. Hubert. The mornings were chilly. We would sometimes go out to hunting blinds, and sometimes we would ride horses. At precisely nine, we would be at Trois-Fouinots, a glorious clearing in the forest where we'd planned our rendezvous. The trees there are giant; it's part of the protected reserve set aside by the government for the navy. If you've never seen it, you would have no idea of the magnificence of nature.

This is where we'd meet up. Three houndmen waited at the corners of the crossroads, each with a pack of twenty dogs. Four servants had saddled horses in hand, all wearing Robert's coat of arms. All the keepers were brought around the fire that had been made for us. We warmed up as we waited for the report.

Eight roads came together at the roundabout. Everyone looked to see if they could spot the keeper coming down one of them. Robert, like in "Bluebeard," kept saying, "Don't you see anyone coming?" Finally, one of the guards answered, "There's Pinoteau." That was our first keeper. All the dogs pricked their ears and stood at attention, as if they understood what was about to be said. Pinoteau arrived and pulled up his scouting dog on its leash.

"Do you have anything good to report?" Robert said.

Pinoteau shook his head sadly. "Monsieur le comte knows that I do what I can, and that when I'm not satisfied, it's not my fault." Pinot always said these things. "I don't have anything good to report. It rained overnight, so everything is wet. I found a herd of wild boar, but my dog lost them. I found the footprint of a boar where he had spent the night, then left early in the morning for the side of the road by Saint-Maur."

"Fine," said Robert with a frown, "if La Feuille" (the assistant groundskeeper) "has no better information than you, I won't hunt."

A few minutes later, La Feuille arrived.

"Anything good?" said Robert.

"Count, I've found one 250-pound boar in the bog behind the guard house. My dog was cutting my hands with his leash as he followed it toward Ardentes. I surveyed the area, and I'm sure it hasn't escaped."

Robert jumped onto his horse. "Raise the alarm," he said, "set the dogs to attack! Look to your packs!"

At this moment, all the dogs began to howl impatiently. The keepers lashed them with a whip, and the pain made them switch to plaintive yelps, but still they yipped even more. Robert waved to me and signaled that I should follow him, so I did.

What a crude pastime this is! Poke around beneath the woods, plunge into the ditches where my horse was in water up to her belly, get hit in the chest by branches. Certainly there's an intoxicating moment when you're in the hunt at full speed and the dogs are in full voice. This unmatched music pulls you in. But when the dogs lose the scent or change direction, it loses its charms.

My initial enthusiasm for the hunt cooled a little, and I started to reflect that this was a dangerous hobby. I could be killed. Robert was ecstatic; he thought of nothing, not even of me behind him. I would go so far as to say, since I was not trying to speak to him or distract him, that he willfully lost me. Finally, that night, they'd cornered the monster, but it had not gone down easy. It had killed four dogs and wounded six.

We went inside, fully fatigued. I wept for the dogs. I was horrified by both the hunt and the boars and the rivalry between them. I told you that jealousy is not the least of my faults.

31

The Winter Garden—Richard

THESE LARGE EXPEDITIONS INTO THE forest took place three times a week. For a while I went along so I wouldn't have to be alone, but that was definitely too hard on a woman. Because of my health, I was forced to give it up. My life went back to being bleak, and I could see that yet again my happiness was about to leave me. Robert would not sacrifice one hour of his happiness for me.

I spent almost all my days and evenings alone in the grand salon, where the wind whistled through every opening. Many times I said to Robert, "My friend, I'm bored. Couldn't you stay in with me more often? I don't like the countryside; I'm used to noise, to the bustle of

Paris. I must love you very much to live here. I know that you can't live in Paris because you don't have enough money. If spending time here saves you money, then I'll be patient. But the hunts that you put on are ridiculously expensive. I don't seem to factor into your life, so I'm telling you that I have made a great sacrifice for you in remaining here. It's not in my character, and the isolation is making me antisocial."

"Why do you stay here? Am I keeping you here by force? I love the hunt, and I'll hunt as much as I like. Anyone who doesn't like it is free to leave. As for these observations, I'm not asking for them. Even if someone in my family were to say anything, I would no longer see them. I know perfectly well what I'm doing and where I'm going. If I'm wasting my money, I'm not asking for anyone's input."

I left the salon and went back to my room in tears. He'd never spoken to me that way.

With my personality, if the joys were vivid, the sorrows were great. He had said this to me in front of ten guests. The only choice I had was to leave the next day. I got my things ready for departure. My heart was shredded. I looked for what I'd done wrong to justify his reaction and found nothing.

He came into my room and said in astonishment, "What is going on with you?"

"You can see what's going on. I've packed my trunks, and I'll leave tomorrow."

"Leave! Why?"

"Because—and it makes perfect sense—you're pushing me toward the door. We're not married, and I'll tell you again: Running the house this way will ruin you. You can't go on like this without joining with another estate. You have to marry. Then you can come back to me when my life as a courtesan is finally over. You've shown me heaven only to throw me into hell. How easily we rise from misery to grandeur, but to descend from grandeur to misery is painful. When you have a heart, it hurts. You've made it very clear today that I am a guest in your house; that's not generous. It was a fatal idea for you to bring me here. You were wrong to do it, and you've shown me the secrets and happiness of a life I should never have known. Everything here became important to me. It's crazy what a person will allow themselves to get attached to. What an idiot, who thinks herself worthy of pity if, after having spent some years here, she's chased out to make room for another! Look at yourself, sad girl, look at your past. It shadows you!

"You're right, Robert. I'm right too. I don't like the countryside. It's a tomb for my sense of fun. When I don't laugh, I think, and when I think, I cry. What kind of interest do you want me to take in all the things surrounding me? The fact that the poplars grow and make twenty sous a year? Get married. While you hunt, this will keep your wife amused. Me, I love balls, the theater—I want to go out. I'm crying, not because I'm sorry I met you, it's just… Ah! I don't know why I'm crying."

"You're crying because you have weak nerves. I don't understand a word of what you just said. I don't want to do anything to hurt you. If I have, I'm sorry. But you don't have to yell at me. I love you, you know that. Often I'm down, I have regrets, and then you tell me all that's in your heart, and I'm turned around. I brought you here to get you away from that scene in Paris. I had you sleep in my mother's room—you, Céleste, who turns white at seeing your past reflected in the mirror! Forgive me for saying so, but that is a sacrilege. You have good qualities. But you are *you*! My family has been in revolt ever since they found out that you're here with me. A day doesn't go by that I don't receive letters demanding your banishment. I don't have the heart. You are my weakness. I think of what I am and what I could have been if I hadn't met you. If I had any regrets, I forgot them when I kissed you. Don't hurt me. Stay with me, and don't be sorry. No one loves you more than me. You miss Paris, so we'll go in a few days. I myself have business interests that take me there. Come on, unpack your trunks. Come back to life without thinking about tomorrow."

I was somber for a few days. I still had troubles. Marie, the maid I'd had for so long, ran off with Robert's valet. He knew about it and asked me to go get her. I did, but I didn't want to. My life became small. I shut myself in and no longer did any needlework. I chastised myself for staying.

"Come on," Robert said, "get your things ready. We'll spend a month in Paris. I've received letters about my business."

I went to hug Justine. I was going to visit my poor mute friend who had begun to get to know me. I said my goodbyes to everything and everyone, because I thought I would never return.

On the way to the city, Robert told me that he couldn't stay at my place because he'd brought along his chef and valet.

"Have you already found—"

"I wrote, and an apartment is being held for me in Antin. I'm going down there."

He'd kept all this from me. There was an ulterior motive for this trip.

"Look, Robert, tell me the truth. You don't know how to lie, you're too loyal. Why are you coming to Paris?"

"I'm going to Paris because you want to go there, Céleste. I don't want to be apart from you, but I must. My family wants me to be seen in society. You'll be at the ball with your people. When people see us without each other, they'll think we've broken up. But you'll secretly come to my place every night. You must set up your life at your place, including hiring a maid. Here's some money, and I'll give you a hundred francs a week."

My blood boiled. This was still a breakup.

"Fine! I'll do as you say. There's a ball at the Winter Garden Saturday, so I'll go."

I had asked for a servant who also knew how to make dresses. One was sent to my apartment, and I looked at her uneasily.

"Do you know how to work, to do dresses? I anticipate having a lot of work for you. When I went to the countryside, I had nothing to wear, and now I'm going to a ball on Saturday."

She was not chatty. "If madame would give me a chance, she'll see that I can put something together."

When we'd settled on a price, I hired her and said, "Could you start right away?"

"Oui, madame."

"Good. Make me this black crepe dress with five swags of pleated fabric, and on each one, three little satin ribbons."

I ordered a crown of golden honeysuckle with green leaves. This look was original and had something sad about it that harmonized with my heart.

Robert watched me dress, and I hoped that he would be jealous, that he would stop me from going out. He didn't do a thing.

"Wait, you're missing something," he said, and he gave me a small box containing a magnificent diamond cross.

I took it joylessly, though it was quite lovely. This was a goodbye gift.

"You look charming. You'll turn all their heads. Have fun. Did you like the bouquet I sent? Save me a place in your mind in the midst of the whirlwind you're about to join."

"Do you want me to not go?"

"No, go. First, I'm sure you'll have fun, and second, you have to be seen on your own. Have you gotten in touch with your friend? Is she coming to take you?"

"Non, I'm going to meet her."

"Then I'll drive you to her place."

When we got to Victorine's door, he didn't say a word. He definitely didn't love me anymore. This was a polite breakup.

He kissed me and drove on, saying, "Until tomorrow."

As I entered Victorine's house, I began to cry.

"Oh my God," she said, "these tears, this black dress—are we going to a funeral? I was going to wear a bright-red velvet dress. I'll change into something gray. You're passing half your grief onto me."

"Don't laugh, my dear. I feel terrible. Robert left me. He's getting married."

"When I got your letter yesterday, where you told me that he was absolutely going to go with you to the ball at the Winter Garden, I was doubtful that he'd do something like that. Don't torture yourself. You should still go. You surely didn't hope he was going to marry you? Take someone else to the ball."

"I could never forget him. If you only knew how I love him!"

"That's why he broke up with you."

"Non, his finances are embarrassing."

"Hold on! I thought he was so rich."

"Oui, he is rich, but he has expensive taste and enormous debts. The hunts alone cost a fortune."

"He is rich, and he doesn't stay with you. He's more ambitious than amorous. Pick out some pretty boy whose passions are exactly the opposite, who has more love than ambition, and make a mockery of Robert. He'll be jealous, then he'll either leave you altogether or come back to you."

We went into the Winter Garden. The hall was resplendent with flowers, lights, and diamonds. No one had seen me in a long time, which was a gauge of my success: They were obsessed with me. I didn't want to dance; however, a young man who was tall, blond, thin, and distinguished asked me so insistently that I accepted. Victorine's advice started to fester in my soul. As I crossed the wasteland of my anger, I was born again for my work as a coquette, and happiness was almost able to erase my memory. My dance partner, with the vanity that comes naturally at his age, attributed my indulgence to something else entirely. He overwhelmed me with his tenacity all night. I endured it, hoping that the game would keep him entertained, that he would try to date me, that Robert would notice, and that jealousy would bring him to my feet.

But did the rival that I'd prepared have the requirements to see this delicate mission through?

I assessed him with this in mind, and the result of my examination was that he was a very pretty boy.

Once I was alone, I consulted Victorine.

"How do you like him? Do you think he'll be good enough to make Robert jealous? He's so perfect!"

I couldn't keep from laughing as Victorine proceeded with her examination. She was definitely earning my confidence.

"Certainly," she said, "he is very nice. Robert must see him."

My dancer asked my permission to send me flowers because he had crumpled my corsage as we danced. I didn't exactly say no, which in all possible worlds, I think, is as good as a woman saying yes.

The astute Victorine understood my reluctance. A few minutes later, she'd found a way to work my address into conversation with my lover, who had no doubt of his success. Victorine's patience paid off.

"What a favor I have done for you, my dear! I am bored to death here. I don't know anyone, and I can't gossip about people I don't know."

"You want to leave?"

"Oui," she said, and she enthusiastically jumped up from her seat.

I was so absorbed by the memory of Robert that I didn't think of my beautiful cross necklace, which had drawn envious glances.

Just as we were leaving, a bunch of people were coming in.

"We're leaving just in time," said Victorine. "Look at the hair on those two. Once looks like an herb garden, and the other an ostrich."

"On the other hand, look at how pretty those two are."

Mmes. Doche and Plunket went in, coiffed with

crowns of bundled flowers and wearing cute outfits. Ozy followed them in.

"Oui, they are well-dressed, but the crown doesn't do the nose any favors."

"Oh, don't say that about Mme. Doche. Look at her."

"I don't need to look at her. I've been seeing her for twenty-five years."

⁂

Back at my place, I thought of Berry, where I was so happy at first and then became so sad. "As if this memory is better than the false joy that I came to find," I told myself as I removed my crown. I wanted to cry. The night seemed to go on and on, and I was antsy.

At noon, I received a magnificent bouquet of Parma violets surrounded by camellias, along with a card. It was from my young man from the night before asking to pay me a visit at four o'clock. I hesitated, and then, remembering what Victorine had told me, I said yes.

Robert arrived at two. I blushed as I waited for my bouquet to have its effect on him.

Robert went to the table, read the card, and said, "You know this gentleman? He's the son of an exchange agent. He's nice, but they say he's an idiot. Not your type."

A carriage stopped at the front door. Robert took my bouquet, opened the window, and as if it were the most natural thing in the world, dropped it as if it were an accident. It almost landed on the head of whoever was getting out of the carriage—none other than the young man. He didn't bother to come all the way up. He got back in the carriage and left.

I was enchanted. This hadn't hurt him very much,

and Robert let me see that he still loved me, that he was jealous. That evening, it was he who was going to a ball. With my elbow on the table and my chin in my hand, I watched him get ready with chagrin. In the world he would be entering, there would be such seductive people! Young, rich, beautiful, upstanding. My thoughts were not to take one more step over the threshold of these doors; they were dropped on the carpet where he wiped his feet as he entered. My Robert was so handsome, so elegant, that he would be the center of attention. It made me want to shred everything he put on.

I waited for him. As each carriage passed in the street, I went to the window. When he returned, he chastised me for staying up so late.

***

My maid that I'd hired was short and brunette. She told me she was married to a driver.

One day when she was pinning a corsage on me, I thought she was bigger than before. I said, "Are you pregnant, Caroline?"

She blushed and said, "Non, madame."

I said no more. She worked like a horse, and she was thrifty. I thought she was wonderful.

In all of Robert's comings and goings, there was one mystery: He wrote a lot and received letters that he hid from me. In cases like this, suspicion is torture. It tore me up and made me the most unpleasant of women. I resolved to learn his secrets. While he was at lunch, I took and hid the key to his desk, which he had left behind that day. While I was at his place, I opened the drawer and greedily pulled out his correspondence. I found letters from his family, all speaking of me in offensive terms. They said:

> *Have you ended it with that girl?...I hope that you're not seeing her anymore.... Think of your future.... This time, at least, have the courage of your convictions. We want you to be happy. Mlle. B... doesn't ask any better than to marry you. But she wants to be quite sure that you don't have any unsavory acquaintances. I even think her family is keeping tabs on you; do not go to the house of that woman.*

My heart broke. I knew that they were right, that Robert's love would ebb in the face of these repeated attacks.

In one drawer, I found a letter written by Robert. It wasn't finished; no doubt my arrival had interrupted him. It would surely be addressed to Mlle. B... and would be an answer to some admonishment they'd made to him because of me. It began like this:

> *In asking for the hand of Mlle. B..., I know what I am doing, and I am too honest a man to not fulfill my obligations. As for Mogador, with whom you are obsessed, I meet up with her sometimes. You might have seen me speaking to her in the street. The poor girl does me no harm, and I don't know why I would pass by her without looking at her.*
>
> *You know, my dear, the life of a young man. We invent distractions, and I invented this one for myself. I was wrong, but what do you want? You can't drown former girlfriends. As soon as I am married, I will move out of town with my wife. Make sure that Mlle. B... does*

her part so that she doesn't have to wait for me too long. Like wine, prolonged tests of one's character aren't worth anything. I hope to have an answer tomorrow...

The letter stopped there. My broken heart was deflated by tears, followed by a hate for the world that had snatched him away from me. What had I done to all these people that made them so obsessed with me? Why did they come after me to separate me from Robert? And why didn't he push back? No, he would hang on to me up to the last moment because he couldn't drown me. He led me on and was only waiting for an answer to leave me. Would I wait around for this humiliation? Was I not brave enough to suffer this? Let's go, pride. Wake up!

I put the letters back, closed the desk, and left.

⁂

When I got home, the concierge gave me my key.

"Where's Caroline? Did she go out?"

"Oui, madame, but she isn't coming back. Contractions overtook her. She went to the hospital in faubourg Saint-Honore."

"What? So she was pregnant?"

"Did madame not see her?"

"Non. It's been a month since I asked her about it. I thought she was fat. She told me she'd always been that way, so I let it drop. If she'd have told me, I wouldn't have let her go to the hospital; she could have had the baby here. Do you know which ward she's in?"

"Oui, Sainte-Marie."

"Go find me a carriage. I'm going to see her."

On the way there, I thought of the role I was about

to play. Should I write to Robert? I couldn't tell him that I'd read his letters. He deserved a better explanation. I'd go there that evening as if I knew nothing and wait for him to let me in on his plan.

I found Caroline.

"Are you crazy to take off from my house like that? Why didn't you tell me that about your condition, which is totally natural, especially since you're married?" She blushed, and I continued. "If you're not, I need too much forgiveness myself to not have it for others."

"I'm so lucky. Madame will take me back when I leave here."

"Well, of course, and if you'd told me of your condition in the first place, you wouldn't even be here."

"You are so kind, madame. And if I dare ask…"

"What is it? Dare away."

"Would you be the godmother of my child?"

"I accept with all my heart. When do you think you'll give birth?"

"The doctor said I still have four or five days."

"That gives me time to buy the things you'll need."

Caroline kissed my hands. I left a little lighter due to the happiness that I was able to give this woman.

I headed straight for Victorine's.

"Aha!" she said. "Everyone comes to see me. It's what people need from me. Your love is not going any better? End it for good."

"Oui, that's my plan. Tomorrow it will all be over. I'm not going back to the chateau where I arranged things for my little Justine with such care. She stuck with me in the country. They'll burn all the needlework I did, and he'll send me money for my furniture. He'll have the right to sell it on to someone else. They'll open the windows so that my impure breath can be aired out. My God! But it all makes sense, so why am I so upset? My heart feels like it's being squeezed by a cobra that sucks out my blood and replaces it with venom. No one has done me any wrong, and yet I want to get revenge. I hate the universe, and I hate myself. You're right, they'll get over it quickly. I'm done living. My heart no longer perks up. Let's go out, we have to! There's a ball at the Winter Garden. Will you come with me?"

Victorine put on her most serious face. "My dear, anything you want, but not that. Balls bore me to death. First, my small income doesn't allow me to follow all the crazy trends of the day. As for you, my dear Céleste, who lived two years of that chateau life, what do you have? Jewels and lace won't keep you warm for very long when times are tough. Believe me, spend less on frivolities, and go to fewer balls."

"Do you think I'm going for fun? Non, it's a necessary distraction from Robert. I need to be talked about, adored, lavished. Come tomorrow; it'll be the last time I ask you. When you come to stay at my place, I won't bother you anymore."

"In that case, I'll allow it. I'll even give you a ride and try to put an end to all this so that I don't have to watch you cry anymore. It makes you ugly, which is no fun for me. I'm too empathetic."

That evening, I dined at Robert's. As usual, I did everything I could to get him to talk about his future plans. He didn't tell me anything as his valet prepared his clothing.

"Are you going out tonight, Robert?"

"Oui, I'm going to a society engagement."

The evening passed without either of us saying

another word to the other. When his carriage pulled away, I began to write a long letter that I planned on burning. It would be better to tell him all this… I'd never had so little courage. I was about to cause our breakup. The very idea made me lose my mind and seemed impossible to do. It was three in the morning. I strode up and down the salon floor. My mind was on fire. These hours seemed to last a lifetime. I envisioned him at a ball, alongside whoever he would marry, smiling at her, saying to her, "I love you!" I projected my hate to come between them, like a vengeful fury. My heart was a lantern, and my blood fell inside it, drop by drop, caught fire, and sent a plume of black smoke to my brain that clouded my sanity. I wanted to kill myself at his house. I said to myself, What's keeping him from loving someone else? The next day, he won't think of me. He won't love me anymore. He'll push me aside so he can keep his self-respect. And then, if his plans to marry fail, if he is rejected, everyone will say, "He cared so little for marriage that he didn't leave his mistress." I'm his backup. Beware, Robert, I hope you suffer like I suffer. I've been abandoned by God, and I must bear this grief.

A carriage stopped outside. It was him!

I pressed my hand against my heart to stop its hammering. It was making me nauseous.

Robert came in, seeming happy. Surely he'd received good news—he hoped. His happiness made me furious.

"Why aren't you in bed?" he asked. "You're pale. Are you sick?"

"Oui, I'm sick. I have a fever. But my illness can be cured in telling you… Mlle. B…, did she say yes? Are you pleased? Is she pretty? How can you love her?"

He blanched but said nothing.

"Tell me that you love her! Why act out this awkward scene with me? Do I wish her ill? You took up with me, and you have the right to leave me. Why are you just standing there? Do I have to wait in your foyer for someone else to enter before I leave, possibly after you've extended your gracious politeness toward me? I don't want anyone's leftovers, and I don't want anyone to steal so much as a thought from me. You displaced me a few days ago when you shared your love with someone else. You have the right to take your love from me, so keep it. You should know that I've already got proof. I won't impose on you, I won't stand in your way. Why not just say it? Do you doubt my resolve? Is this silence to spare me? It's not working. Direct hits heal quickly. Come on, say something."

"I don't know who you saw and who sparked your imagination, my poor Céleste. You're not making sense. You know my position, my wealth, my family, but you don't at all understand the rules of that world. I gave in to my parents' wishes, whose most cherished wish was to see me settled. I've not spoken to you of these new plans because they could easily fall through, and I recoiled at the idea of causing you needless pain. If I had known it would hit your heart as hard as it hit your head, I would have told you everything the first day."

"If they're going to drown the girls you've known, that be easier to take. No explanations necessary."

"You read letters not meant for you to see. You often forget exactly who you are, Céleste. Don't make me regret what I've done for you. Your heart is good, but your lack of education makes you do and say inconvenient things. Next time, be aware that letters not addressed to you are sacred, and even if you know where they are kept, you should respect that. I have your furniture at my house in the country. If I marry, I will pay you for it; I'll give you twenty thousand francs. You're afraid of the future, and this will be the seed of a small fortune. We won't see each other anymore, but I promise to hold good memories of you."

The night was late, and I put on my coat to leave.

"Not even a handshake, Céleste?"

"Fine."

His hand was icy. Like me, all the blood was in his heart.

To talk about tears so often is tiring, but that's what comes with so much sadness. I cried until noon, when I was brought a letter and a package. It contained the things I'd left at Robert's. The note only had these lines:

As soon as I receive a little money, I'll send it to you. Now and forever, I'll lie awake and think of you.
Robert

That night, when Victorine came looking for me, I was not ready. She dressed me with the efficiency of a mason building a wall and got me to the ball. I wore a white lace dress and an updo with pomegranates. My outfit was lovely and, above all, light.

"Come on, move past your regrets. You are ravishing. Truly, I thought you were stronger than this."

"I don't have the strength on the first day. The wound is deep, my love is gone. He broke me into little pieces by leaving."

We arrived, and the party was more brilliant than the first time. I danced closely with my partners for the benefit of my pretend sister. When I say dance, I mean be face-to-face with one person and then another because it was so packed you couldn't actually move.

Victorine was in a very good mood. She laughed and said, "I'm dancing! It's been years! Céleste's sadness made me get up."

After about two hours, the crowd thinned a little. The ball became more animated and lively. I felt the dark cloud of sadness that had overtaken my heart begin to evaporate. Dancing always held an irresistible charm for me. I breathed in the joyful fanfares from the orchestra and for once I didn't miss a waltz, a polka, or a mazurka.

There were many stage artists there. Hyacinth made enough noise for four people. They pressed around him, and he displayed his huge nose and huge hands for all to see. He dispensed his wisdom, as these authors regularly asked him to. His director didn't like his showing up there. He'd have preferred to keep his performances to the stage. Everyone surrounded him and pressed in to hear him. He was gay and funny as a child as he followed after a woman in her forties who was alone and dressed horribly. He kept calling her Elvira and said, "Dance with me. I love you, madame. Don't be cruel, or I'll poke you with my nose."

Grassot, who is always the same, was also insane and funny. He cavorted around the women, stopped at the prettiest ones, took them by the arm, and spoke to them as if he knew them.

A quadrille began. I stationed myself at the other end of the hall. We had made a figure and were waiting for our turn to come when I heard my name—very loud.

"Wait, that's Mogador! Look how beautiful she is!"

"You think so?" said another voice. "I don't understand how anyone finds that woman beautiful. She's the exact opposite."

I peered to see who would put me down like that. It was the loveliest boy you've ever seen in your life.

"In the end," said the one who'd spoken first, "you couldn't take what looks she has away from her. You don't think she's beautiful, but this doesn't erase her lovely arms, her small waist, her height, her figure, her beautiful hair, her pretty eyes, and the white teeth of a puppy."

"It's possible," said my detractor. "I didn't look at her."

"You're being an ass."

If only I could have given as good as I'd gotten to this fine, indifferent young man! It would have been satisfying to find him ugly, but to be fair, he was not in the least.

The only thing you could say about him was that he was too beautiful for a man. After all, I told myself, people are free. All the same, if you're a little bit of a coquette, it's vexing to know that someone finds you horrifying without having bothered to look at you. As soon as the dance was over, I ran to Victorine.

When I found my young man again, I walked past him ten times. I made the rounds like a peacock. I wanted my enemy to see me. He seemed entirely occupied with a woman who was not pretty at all.

I took the hint and was about to move away when the shorter man, who was his cousin, stopped me and said, "Mademoiselle, you dance ravishingly. If I weren't such a bad dancer, I'd ask you."

"Well, monsieur, ask me. Maybe you don't know how good you are."

He offered his arm, beaming. "I accept with pleasure."

I hoped that his friend was about to follow. Not at all. As we danced, I said, "You were wrong to not dare ask me to dance. I owe you for the way you defended me. This gentleman over there does not like me at all. He doesn't want you to give me the time of day."

"Oh! You heard that? How awkward. He doesn't know what he's saying."

"Why say anything then? He's probably right to think I'm ugly. To each his own, but to come at me with hate!"

"What madness, madame. Until he is sorry that his silly words reached your ears, I am going to pummel him for you. He must come over and apologize."

I wanted to hold him back, but he escaped.

A pantomime played out on the far side of the hall. I could see the other man defending himself, but the short one was stubborn and made my case to him.

He was a young man; he couldn't have been more than twenty-two or twenty-four. He was tall, a bit muscled, but well formed. His blond hair and sideburns framed his flat, white face. His moustache left his mouth exposed, and his lips were a little thick but well made, with white teeth. He had a lopsided smile, which created a dimple in his cheek and made him gorgeous. He had a narrow nose, a charming face, and the sweetest eyes in the world. He was distinguished and elegant, with the hands and feet of a Creole. What he had turned every woman's head. They saw him, and they followed him. Poor Richard!

I'll say it again: He was too beautiful for a man.

He came over to me.

Victorine, who'd neither seen nor heard anything of this little scene, nudged my arm and said, "Look at that pretty boy!"

"Oui, he's coming to talk to me. He's my enemy."

"What a shame! If he had just inclined himself your

way a little, this one could have made Robert die of jealousy."

He had reached us and seemed very embarrassed.

"My God, monsieur, do I displease you so much that you've lost the ability to speak?"

"Not at all, mademoiselle. I'm asking you to believe that when I spoke of you so badly an hour ago, it's because I hadn't seen you. You must forgive me. I'm a lazy Creole, but you are very charming. I'm here with my whole heart to make honorable amends."

"Be careful, monsieur, you're sitting on my dress. It's lace, and you're not light."

"Oh! Sorry! I'm clumsy. Can I fix it?"

"Not at all, monsieur. I share your opinion of my kind of beauty, which I heard perfectly well. So don't trouble yourself in looking for compliments to flatter me. I'm surprised by your opinion of my appearance, Creole though you may be, which you wouldn't have said if you thought I could hear."

"I want to convince you that my repentance is equal to my crime. I'm most sincere in my retraction. You are very attractive, first of all. Nothing touches me more than the sound of your voice. I love the sound of your voice. And you have such lovely hands! I'm crazy not to have seen all this. I got off to such a bad start with you to ever dare hope, but I would be glad to become your friend."

"Non, monsieur. I would lose still more in your opinion, since my moral self is even worse than the physical. Adieu; I'm going to dance."

He stood there, thinking.

A half hour later, the little gentleman who was his cousin came up to me and said, "What did you do to Richard? Pardon me for what I'm about to say, but I think he lost his head this evening in every sense. Now he's mad about you. He says that you're magnetic, that you've thrown him to his fate, that there is only you, the most beautiful woman in the world, and he absolutely must see you again."

"Ah, that! He thinks he hurt me with his opinion of me, which he delivered so badly. Reassure him that it no longer crosses my mind. I have other things to keep in my head."

As we talked, Richard chatted with Victorine, and then it was time to leave. He asked permission to take me home. I thanked him and said we would go our separate ways.

"He is charming," Victorine said, following him with her eyes. "It's necessary, my dear, to turn the proverbs to your own uses. In your case, the ebb and flow. We've gone to two balls, you've had two conquests. It seems right," she said with a laugh, "that this adventure began like the other one. Let's wait until the end of the ball; if you go now, I'll be alone and horribly bored. I don't need to tell you that he asked me for your address."

A premonition squeezed my heart.

"You didn't give it to him, I hope."

"Of course I did. You needed a distraction, and here's a good one—and, I'm sure of it, sweet revenge."

"Oui, you're right. But he won't come. He only did all of that to be polite."

"He won't come!" said Victorine, ringing the bell as we went through the door. "Rest assured that you'll see him at four o'clock tomorrow. Good night. If you don't have anything better to do, come dine with me tomorrow."

I got back to my house half asleep. As I picked up my

flowers, I thought of Robert.

Victorine was right. This adventure had begun like the other. It wouldn't have the same ending at all, I told myself. What if Richard is falling in love with me? He is handsome, as handsome a man as maybe Mlle. B… is a pretty woman! If one day we were to go out together, and if I met Robert while I was on Richard's arm, and he saw that I was not abandoned and alone, and that I didn't only love him because I needed him. M. Richard is not noble; I know who he is. But who cares! He is so elegant, so distinguished. Let's see if he shows up.

And I fell asleep.

This show of a desire would create misfortune for all three of us. Who would have thought that a word uttered thoughtlessly in the chaos of a party could extend its influence over a whole lifetime.

32

Cholera—My Goddaughter

I GOT UP EARLY AND went to see Caroline in the hospital. She had gone into labor, and they placed a little girl in my hands, so tiny, so delicate, that I said to myself, *She won't live long.*

This was what the doctor thought too, because he asked me if I would go hold her over the baptismal font.

"Oui, doctor."

"Good. We have time to quickly baptize her."

"But I don't have another godparent here. And I want to do the baptism at the church of Roule. It can wait until tomorrow morning."

The nurse said to me, "But madame, there's a chapel here. One of the orderlies will be the godfather."

I was on the verge of accepting, despite my disgust. The idea that this child had been born and that she would be baptized at the hospital depressed me, but time was short, so I was about to say yes. Then the little girl began to cry and squirm with a vigor I hadn't thought she was capable of. It seemed as if she was saying to me, "I will wait until tomorrow." The father was there, and he asked me to let the little one stay with one of his friends, whom he would bring along.

"I'll be here tomorrow at ten a.m.," I said.

M. Richard kept his word. At four o'clock, he was at my place. I teased him very much about his change of heart. I asked him if he followed politics.

"You are naughty!" he said. "Do you always want me to act like that toward you?"

"Me! I assure you I do not."

"Great. Come dine with me tomorrow, with your friend and my cousin. It's the only way you'll be able to persuade me that you're not holding a grudge against me."

"You are very kind. I don't hold a grudge against you, but I can't accept. I have a lot to do; I'm a godmother now."

"You'll be free by six. I'll come get you."

"Non, you will send me your cousin while you go fetch Victorine."

"You're not being straight with me; you're hiding something."

"Non, non. But do as I say, or I won't go."

"Since that's an order, I will obey. Adieu."

The next day at nine o'clock, I was at the hospital with my little parcel. I dressed my goddaughter, and everything I'd bought was too big. I had to use pins on her little bonnet.

As we entered the church, my heart stopped. A beautiful marriage ceremony was taking place. I thought of Robert, and two tears fell from my eyes onto the forehead of the little girl in my arms. I wiped them off. This first taste of water that had fallen on the head of this little angel before her baptism was impure. When it was our turn, I went up to the priest, who anointed her with holy water.

When he told me that my obligation was to serve as her mother if she were orphaned, I promised. I gave her the name Solange in memory of Berry, so that she might remember for me. As we left the church, I clutched her against my heart. I wanted to run off with her; it was as if she were mine. I thought of her mother, who was waiting for her, and I took the path to the hospital. I put her back in her crib with regret. She needed a wet nurse, so I gave myself the job of finding one. I didn't come back to see her until two days later.

⁂

Robert had left town. He didn't even try to come see me. I didn't try to find him either, but I was miserable.

I found Caroline pale, with haunted eyes. When she saw me, she sat up and said, "Did you find a wet nurse?"

"Yes, she's coming tomorrow."

"Oh, madame, we don't need her to come tomorrow; we need her today. Death is in the room. Since you were here last, five women and four babies have died. Look around—there will be another death today. I'm afraid. I beg you to take my child."

I thought that milk fever had gone to her brain.

"Calm down, don't torture yourself. There's no danger. Tomorrow isn't that far off."

"Just look around you, madame."

She fell back. I crossed the ward and saw something truly frightening: a young woman, probably twenty-two, held a newborn in her arms. She tried to hold him to her breast, but he refused. She was blonde, and the skin on her chest was white, but her face was violet. She was apparently in a lot of pain as she cried and adjusted him. I turned away. I stopped a young nurse who was on her rounds, and I asked her what was going on. She raised her gaze to heaven in answer.

"Wait," I said to her as I slid five francs into her hand. "Take good care of that woman." I pointed to Caroline.

"Are you the godmother of her daughter? Get her out of here quickly. If you can, get her mother out too! But it won't matter." She left me to go care for the sick.

"You saw?" Caroline said to me when I returned to her bedside.

"Oui, but it's not contagious."

"Non, madame, non. It's something out of the ordinary. Take my daughter, as you promised. As soon as I can be put in a carriage, I'll be at your place."

"Of course, but there's no need to worry. I'll take Solange. The wet nurse wagon, on rue de la Victorine, goes out every three days. I'll keep her at my place. You stay calm, okay? I'll come back tomorrow to see you."

She thanked me with a wave, and I carried away this poor little creature, light as a feather, certain that I was saving her from death. I handed her over to the wet nurse as if she were my own daughter. It was a woman from Guise who was very clean. She gave me confidence. I was put at ease by the little one, who was full of life. She was not troubled, and I hadn't heard her cry once.

While attending to Caroline, I had hired a German woman to work at my house during the day. She was a worker, and she did everything without complaint.

This was March 19, 1849. On this day, the Beaujon Hospital was in chaos. They emptied the rooms, and the pregnant women, who were in wards on the ground floor, were moved up to the second. Everything was scrubbed and neat as a pin. However, despite these precautions, death strode in with giant steps and reaped a terrible harvest. Since Caroline's admission, seventeen women and children had died almost instantly. Mortality was twice as bad for women waiting to give birth. Poor Caroline, on seeing me, got back her color. She was happy.

I told her, "Our girl is fine. How are you doing?"

"Better. We no longer have any fresh air here. You can see that it's always dirty. Leave—I'm sure it's the plague."

"Don't give yourself such ideas. It'll slow your recovery."

To reassure her, I took a tour of the room and stopped at each bedside. What I had heard about cholera seemed to match what I saw. I found an intern and begged him to tell me plainly what he knew.

"Well, mademoiselle, if you value the life of this poor woman, get her out, even though she's only been here nine days. We're concealing the frightening news as much as possible, but there's no use in pretending anymore. It's cholera."

"Tomorrow her husband will bring her to my place. Get him to sign her out."

This news perked Caroline up. She had been scared, and this was causing half her illness.

The next day, a cart stopped at my door. I opened the window and saw Caroline. Her husband carried her in. I was taken aback by how much she had changed. Her eyes were sunken, her cheeks lined, her lips black. I had her lie in my bed while I went out fetch my doctor—Robert's doctor. The little one would leave the next day. I changed out the room.

The doctor looked at Caroline a long time and said to me, "Get the child out without her seeing. It can't come near her bed."

You couldn't bring an infant near her mother without her kissing the baby.

I searched for what I could do. "Adèle," I said to my German maid, "go find me powdered camphor."

When she returned, I put some in my little goddaughter's clothing, in her cap, in her swaddling, and I gave her to her mother so she could say her goodbyes.

Caroline took her in her arms, held her tightly against her chest, touched her lips to her face, and then fell still.

I shook all over. Her feverish breath could surround the baby and poison her. I leaned over the bed and took the baby back.

"You're going to suffocate her. She's mine too." Caroline released her.

She let me take her without resisting. The infant was taken out, and I felt more at ease.

I went to stay the night at Victorine's.

My doctor came twice a day. He took me aside the third day and said, "She's a lost cause. As soon as her husband is here with her, go to your friend's. You'll make yourself sick."

"My dear doctor, don't worry about me. If I were worth something, there would be a danger, but I'm not worth anything, so there's nothing to fear. Besides, if there was an exception for me, that would be a great favor granted by God. Are you sure, doctor, that there's no more to be done? She has a baby. Call on all your science, have one of your colleagues come, but save her."

"I've done all I can do. There's no more hope."

I left this poor woman that evening at six o'clock to go to Victorine's. I dreamed of Caroline all night. She was getting better, and she came looking for me. At seven a.m., I got up.

"What are you going to do at your house?" Victorine said. "You have plenty of time before you head over."

"Non, I have to go. Two hours ago I heard someone call my name. It's probably because it's all I can think about, but it woke me up."

As I went up rue Amsterdam, which led to my place, I ran into a little actress named Virginie Mercier, who I had known at Délassements and then at Vaudeville. After asking how she was, I told her, "You've found me on a sad day. I'm going back to my house shaken up because I'm afraid death is there, and I told him where I am."

"Would you like me to go with you?"

"You would be doing me a huge favor."

When I entered my place, Caroline was stiff and her eyes were closed. The German girl signaled to me that she thought it was all over, but two hours later the sick woman asked for me.

"I want to see madame," she said, "go find her!" And she let out a loud cry.

I approached the bed and spoke her name. Her body shifted, her eyes opened halfway, and they turned toward me.

"Would you like to make confession?"

"Non, madame. They offered to send one." She wept.

I took her hand and said, "Caroline, do you hear me?"

She nodded.

"Good, my dear. You asked for me; what would you like me to do?"

She pushed down her blanket without a word and showed me her hand. Her fingers were lifeless. There was a great fire in the fireplace. I asked for cloths and warmed them, with Virginie's help, and put them on Caroline's feet, on her stomach and chest. We changed them out often.

Caroline made a movement like she was feeling better, and her eyes never left mine. She warmed up little by little, and her words came back to her.

"My good lady, I waited for you."

"I'm here, and I won't leave you again. But I am going to bark at you a little. Why haven't you wanted to see a priest? Are you afraid?"

"Oui."

"Why? Their words are comfort and chase away evil spirits. I want to find one, do you hear me? We'll pray together."

Her husband heard, and he was about to go to the church. She looked at all of us, threw me a kiss, and said to me, "You'll take care of my baby girl, yes? *She only has you.*"

"Oui, I will take care of her, and you too. You'll be better tonight. Here's your husband."

She tried to give me a sign, but I didn't understand.

When I brought the priest, he spoke to her, and she murmured, "Oui."

Virginie and I got to our knees at the end of the bed.

During the prayer, Caroline had a seizure. Her body almost rolled onto the floor, but we caught her. She wanted to speak, but cramps twisted her limbs. She became contorted, then fully extended, and fell back with her mouth and eyes open.

I thought I saw a mist pass by. It was the passing of her soul!

Everyone said their prayer, and Virginie took her leave. Caroline's husband went out with the priest, and I remained alone with the dead. I put my right hand on her still-warm forehead and my left on my heart, and I vowed to raise her daughter, to watch over her and make her an honest woman, because I knew her father would do nothing. He wasn't actually married to Caroline; he was married to another woman. Without me, the poor baby only had the orphanage.

The body of the dead decomposed so quickly that no one wanted to sit vigil. They said her husband, to forget his grief, had gone to the cabaret. I sat vigil by myself. I spent the night reading in the next room.

When they came to get her, I accompanied her to the church on rue Caumartin. I left her at the threshold. She could read what was in my heart and go in peace, sure that her daughter would be happy.

33

Indecision

I GAVE NOTICE TO MY landlord, since my lodgings were inconveniently located. I rented no. 24 boulevard Poissonière, a nice little apartment on the second floor facing the front of the building. My plan was to return to the theater, and Richard came to see me sometimes.

After I moved, I found out what had become of Robert. He had left for Vendée to stay with a family member.

Did Richard really love me? I made him prove it over and over. I needed to believe in affection from someone, and that was the power he held over me. He was extremely sweet and consistently loving. One thing bothered him: I always talked about Robert. Sometimes I did it without thinking, and sometimes I was thinking of him more than ever. But I couldn't stop myself.

I didn't know just what position Richard held in society. Some said he was very wealthy, but others said it wasn't so much. Since he held himself in high regard, he could be exaggerating.

I furnished my dining room in antique chestnut and found a magnificent bed. The rest of my things were sent from Berry. Richard sent his upholsterer with orders to put anything I needed on his account. Paris is a marvelous city! And two days later, my apartment was decorated.

For all these favors, Richard received a meager thank you: a smile. I was depressed. My love for Robert was my master; I gave up on the pointless struggle. I tried to forget with all my might, but the memory did me in and left me to die. I searched in vain for a way out. Robert was one of those men who did everything well, who made everyone happy. He was a perfect gentleman in the smallest of ways: good, generous, brave, quick-witted, frank. Everyone loved him—me more than any of them. My passion colored everything about him, but those who knew him know that I'm not exaggerating.

Richard had great qualities, but he showed none of that sort of exuberance and imagination. He was sweet and kind.

Not long after I'd settled in, he came looking for me one evening to ask me to dinner. We were at leaving my building when I saw Robert.

He stopped, looked at Richard, and said to me, "Could I have a word with you?"

His stern expression made me fall to pieces. I shook, not knowing how to answer.

"Okay then," Robert said, "have you decided?"

I looked at Richard, who didn't know Robert, but

he figured it out. He was livid. I pleaded with him with my eyes and said to him, "Would you so be so kind as to wait for me at Maison d'Or? I'll meet you there in five minutes."

"Of course," Richard said to me while looking at Robert. Robert looked back at him defiantly. Their eyes locked with sparks of violence.

"Go," I said, pushing Richard a little. "I promise."

He turned and walked away. Robert folded his arms and followed him with his eyes. Then he turned to me and said, "I am crazy about you, my dear. I am out of my mind, but I came as soon as I could, and it wasn't soon enough. He's fine, this gentleman. You didn't waste any time. I need to speak to you of practical matters, but you're busy. I can go. I should have known that when you leave a woman like you alone for a few hours, you have to put it in writing that you would rather not meet her with other men. And with Mogador, every second counts."

I felt sarcasm coming on, and I willed it to stop.

"Wasted time, Robert, that's what I spent and what I still spend on loving you. I contorted myself to accept the situation, and in exchange I hoped that you'd never come here to insult me. I never did anything to you. You took up with me, and then you dropped me. I suffered then and I suffer still, yet I never voiced a single complaint against you or berated you. I don't have a fortune, but I would have rather died than ask you for anything."

"Charming! It's out of affection for me that you accept the favors of another. So you don't love him, this other man?" Robert's voice became quiet, and he looked sad.

"Non, I'm sorry to say."

"Wonderful. Stay with me. Don't go to dinner. You owe me that; I'm all out of sorts because I'm unable to spend time with you. But if you leave, I'll go and never see you again."

"I'll always love you, Robert. What you came here to say doesn't exactly make me happy, but at the price you've just set, I cannot accept. It would be terribly rude if I don't go see M. Richard. I'm very lucky to have found him. He doesn't cling to me, and I can't be ungrateful. I'm going to go. After dinner, I'll go home and write to him that I can't see him if you promise to never talk that way about me again."

I had said all was going to say. Robert was too smart to not understand that I was right.

"Go," he said. "I'll wait for you."

I arrived at Maison d'Or. Richard let out a cry of joy on seeing me. "I was so afraid you wouldn't come! How did your conversation with M. Robert go?"

"Just as it should have gone—fine. I'm going to see him in a bit, since I still have some business to settle with him."

"What?" said Richard. "Are you going to see him after dinner?"

"Oui, my friend."

"Look, Céleste, don't lie to me. You're leading me to the slaughter, aren't you? You're breaking up with me? It's awful! I don't want to tell you what to do. You've educated me enough regarding his character that I can predict this: He'll make you miserable and leave you again within a month. Come back to me then, to the man who loves you for you and not for my ego. I can't fight him because you love him. I have to resign myself to waiting."

He took my hands, kissed them, and said, "Go, then. Your presence makes it too hard. But don't forget me."

I got into a carriage as he quickly walked away. I

realized that it had been brutal to leave him like this. I had sacrificed too much to Robert.

He welcomed me coldly. He only planned to spend a few days in Paris; he was to leave that same week. He surely had no intention of taking me with him, but events had unfolded to change his decision.

He looked at every little thing in my apartment with a judgmental smirk and told me all of it was in bad taste. I defended what I had been given by Richard.

Robert took it as an insult and got it into his head to bring me a set of emeralds and diamonds fit for a queen. I looked at them in astonishment, not wanting to believe that a treasure like that could be mine. When I came out of my shock, I scolded him.

"I'll never have an occasion to wear such beautiful things, and they are so expensive! This was a mistake; you're upsetting me."

He responded politely that it wasn't about me.

Must I admit that once the first shock passed, I accepted this magnificent gift easily enough? Since then, I have become very blasé about the benefits of coquetry, but I had not yet arrived at this degree of stoicism. Also, to be completely honest, I should say that despite my happiness with the gift, I didn't sleep for two nights. I would wake up with a start, sure that someone had broken in.

This set, which had a bracelet, brooch, earrings, and rings, would have been worth twenty thousand francs from a reliable seller. It had probably cost Robert double that at his jeweler on the Palais-Royal. This man had a habit of marking up everything he sold to Robert, despite his not having a fortune. But Robert never noticed, so the man continued to take advantage. I didn't like the look of him, and I never wanted to deal with him for even the smallest thing. My impression did not steer me wrong: He showed up in my life like the traitor in a play.

Robert was charmed by my enchantment with the jewels, so he said, "Pack your trunks, you're coming with me."

I'm sorry to keep driving you down the road to Berry so often, but I'm obliged to follow the thread of my life. It's not a fault of the narrative that I was embarrassed twenty times in the same location. The legend of my love affair with Robert was a legend of voyages. We embarked from such different points in life that we caused many paths to meet.

I'd been in Berry for two troubled weeks when the same arguments started up again.

"Look, Robert, you're making me unhappy, and you're not happy either. You often say awful things to me without any rhyme or reason. You have regrets, and I'm their cause. Do you want me to go?"

He often answered no, but the next day the arguing would begin again. He hunted more than ever, and his business took more and more of his time. I saw that this was better for him; he seemed more secure. One day, when he returned from the hunt, I complained of being lonely. He had missed his shot, and I paid for his loss.

"Oh, that! My dear, you've retracted your goodwill. You know how I live my life. If I'm making you long for people who are more fun than me, know that I've tried to be kind in return for your sacrifice. If you don't think that's enough, then say the word."

His tone was frightening. I had gotten used to Richard being so sweet. Now I was with Robert, and you quickly get used to whatever's nearby. Richard faded from my thoughts as Robert occupied them more.

I said to Robert, "You gave me beautiful jewelry, and I wear it in the sun so that it dazzles. But that's not enough to keep me busy all day. The things I can do here are so depressing, and this chateau brings bad luck. Your gardener lost both his daughters within a month, and Solange lost her mother. For a few days now, I've been making little mourning dresses for her and her sisters, and it's upsetting to see you. I only hear howling from morning to night—your kennels are full of rage. Every day, you lose one or two of those beautiful dogs, which I practically raised. The wind blows through your ancient towers as if the roofs might lift off. My hatred of the countryside grows, and then you have no idea what's going to happen the next day. I'm always waiting to be taken back to Paris. You can't keep me here for long. You make foolish purchases. Running the house this way will ruin you. You've made me an accomplice in your nonsense by giving me gorgeous jewels. I was happier when I first came here, when you hadn't paid for me, as you put it now. Since we are on the subject, I told you what I needed to be happy with you: lowering your expenses. My love for you, along with encouraging you to rebuild your fortune, would make me happy to stay here as shut in as you like. The first day I met you, I told you I was a courtesan. You knew my past, my hopes for the future, and how I lived every day. You would have given me great pleasure by handing over a quarter of the value of those jewels in cash."

Robert didn't answer at all. Not a word. I'd gotten under his skin. Would this make him decide to leave me again?

Several days went by after this speech. Things were tense.

One morning, I said, "What is going on, Robert? Is there some new plan that's bothering you and you don't want to tell me? My presence here is bothering you."

"Non, Céleste, your presence doesn't bother me, but I have lost a substantial sum in the market. I'm preoccupied."

I always had to pull what he was thinking out of him. When you're jealous, you go looking for the truth until you find it, and then what you find is ten times more depressing than you expected. I often had suspicions, and by pressing him, I gave him an idea that hadn't occurred to him. That's what happened again this time too.

"Oui," I said to him, "maybe you've lost a lot. Only marriage can get you out of this predicament where you find yourself. Don't hold back on my account. Then you can keep this chateau and its grounds, take a fiancée, accept a marriage agreement that would make you a millionaire two times over. Living with me, you'd have to sell all this. I would never ask something so extreme of you. I'm only sorry that you came back to look for me. I should have said no, but what do you want? I still love you. A love like mine isn't worth such a great sacrifice. Think about it."

He held my hands and said, "You're right. I'm a fool. A superb marriage candidate has been proposed. I refused because of you, though you're bored here and would be happier in Paris with the people you love and who support you. What could I do for you? My life is a life of restriction, and you've already been part of that for too long. I grant you your freedom. You may go when you wish."

"Take me to the city tomorrow."

I went back to my room resigned, but as I packed,

a storm gathered in my heart. I had told myself that it was me who wanted to break up, that it was me who was fine with it. The thunder rumbled in my soul, and I said to myself, He should not have accepted. He would be willing to leave it all behind to live with me if he loved me. I refused to go down to dinner.

The next day at ten a.m., I asked how he was feeling.

"How are you this morning," he said to me calmly. Maybe he was faking, but he played it so well that it sent me into a rage.

"You are too okay with this. I'm leaving. You can see that I'm ready. Try to make this breakup our last. Every time we break up, my love shatters and turns to dust. Be sure that your love, if you have any, works like mine, because I would have you suffer just as terribly. My lack of education has left something wild in me that wishes you ill. The day I no longer love you, you will kill yourself at my doorstep, and I will step over your body as I go out. Spare me or never need me. In my world, there are people who have a hatred for and a need for revenge on the people above them. They don't like when 'great' men use their birth and advantages to force their will on others. They get close to people, they take their measure, and if they see that you're below their station, they ask why, especially when the heart and imagination should keep you apart. The one of lower status says to themselves, *Why am I not at their level?* I am lower, Robert. I can only receive and never give. If I were at your level, I would make you very happy, but at mine, everything makes me miserable. The most insignificant word is a wound. You laugh. Does my pride spark your pity? Is it my fault if my soul hasn't lost all its good qualities? One thing remains, and it crumbles in the dust of everything else. I'll wash it with my tears, and it stays with me.

"Adieu, Robert. Remember what I said. If one day you're more unlucky than me, you'll see if I still love you. What separates us is your position in society. I hate it. I want to give you kisses, I don't want to sell them. The love that I have for you can't be bought, not by you, and not by anyone rich enough to pay for it. Adieu! Watch while I leave you without shedding a tear. You call this my self-centeredness, but it's my pride reawakening."

He didn't try to stop me. He did say, I think, adieu as if he was determined to never see me again.

34

THE THEATER DE FOLIES-DRAMATIQUES

I RETURNED TO PARIS DESPERATE as always. I had to find something to do, for my own future and that of my little girl Solange, who I had renamed Caroline in memory of her mother. Whenever I had news of her, she was doing well. This was a relief, but the better she was doing, the more I needed to include her in my plans. I decided to return to the theater and made several fruitless inquiries.

I'd been told to talk to M. Mouriez, director of the Folies-Dramatiques theater, but he had a reputation for being harsh. I didn't dare go looking for him. I decided to write to him instead, telling him who I was and what I wanted. He responded via his manager that he would see me the next day. It's easy for people with a bad reputation to seem charming, and that's what happened with M. Mouriez. I hadn't ever experienced his personality, nor his person, nor his temperament. Everyone knew that he was one of the best people in the theater business in Paris. He brought in plenty of money and paid his artists well, in contrast to many others. His advice, though sometimes terse, was always good. The proof was in the fact that a lot of talented actors and actresses came out of his theater. All the old retired actors spoke well of him and missed him. I am one of them.

I went to his office. He glanced at me sideways and kept writing as he said, "You want to work in my theater?"

"Oui, monsieur, and I'd be very glad if you'd let me."

"Have you ever acted?"

"Oui, monsieur, but very little and very badly. I was in one show at Beaumarchais, and one at Délassements."

"That's not much." He turned to look at me. This examination seemed to go well for me. "You'd be happy enough working here? I should warn you that I have actresses who are doing well. You'll have to work to be perfect."

"If you'll take me on, I promise to be perfect, and I'll try to be good. If you'll give me a try, you wouldn't have to pay me at first." I think my offer offended him.

He jumped out of his chair and said, "Mademoiselle, if it works out, I will hire you and pay you. I don't take anyone on for free. I pay the people who work for me. Yesterday I had the satire *The Wandering Jew* read to me; you'll debut in that. There is a role for the queen of the Bacchanal, would that suit you?"

My answer was a signature at the bottom of the contract he offered me.

"Good," he said. "You'll read the piece later this afternoon."

I left glowing. If you're depressed and counting your woes, when a great joy comes along, you swing far in the opposite direction. I wanted to shout to everyone I passed, "I've got a job at the Folies! They'll pay me, and I've heard they provide the costumes!" But I didn't think this held any interest for the general public, so I went in search of someone to tell.

I was on the boulevard Saint-Denis, where Richard was living. If what he'd said was true, I wouldn't find anyone more interested in me, so I asked if he was in and went up. That gave me time to reflect. Though his apartment was very nice, it was on the fifth floor. By the time I got to the fourth floor, I was afraid he wouldn't be happy to see me. I went back downstairs, saying to myself, I left him so abruptly. He said what everyone says: "You can always count on me."

Let's admit that he had a little bit of a bad time. He would have found many women to console him; maybe at this very moment there was a pretty nursemaid helping him recover in his apartment. I kept going down the stairs. One more flight, and I'd be at the bottom. But I felt my precious contract in my pocket. The need to show it to someone overwhelmed me, and I climbed back up the stairs all the way to the top without stopping for breath. I rang the bell, thinking, What if the woman inside was someone who'd been my friend? But it was Richard who opened the door.

I began to speak fast as a mockingbird. I had so many things to tell him that this went on for twenty minutes without him understanding a word I said. I have to say that he wasn't paying close attention; he stared at me in astonishment.

"This is how you welcome me," I said. "You don't even say hello. I'll go."

He blocked my way and began to laugh. "I didn't say anything because I'm surprised to see you, and because you didn't give me a chance. You didn't stop. Thank you for trusting me enough as your friend to come tell me what has made you so happy."

I was annoyed to be brought up short. He seemed cold, and I felt awkward. I stood up straight and said, "And I thank you for listening to me. I'll go."

He sat me down. "Relax a little, at least, after walking up five floors. Tell me how all this happened. How are you on your own again?"

"It's not hard to figure out. Robert broke up with me, with orders to get out of Berry within twenty-four hours, including the ten hours on the train. I was my weakest self while I was with him. Now that I have a job, my dedication to it will be firm. I will no longer leave the city."

"You," Richard said slowly. "He only has to give you the signal, and you'll go back to him."

"I had heard that you were upset about all this, but you don't love me anymore, do you?"

"I hoped for this, I did everything to make this happen, and now it's my bad luck fairy who's brought you here. If only I hadn't seen you again."

"I understand. I'll go."

"No, I caused you to appear. Let me look at you. I was so unhappy to lose you, it was so difficult."

"You didn't waste away from wanting."

"You're always laughing, Céleste. Look, you're single. I'll forget what you did to me, and we'll remain friends. I think it's a mistake for you to return to the theater. You'll lose more than you'll win."

"You know very well, Richard, that there was a turning point in my life. I am forced to go on carrying this chain without having the power to cut it off."

"If I could throw all my money at it, I would immediately release you from this shame of being on the rolls. Stay with me, be patient, and soon... I can't give you false hope. That would be too cruel."

I couldn't read his mind, and for fear of being wrong, I didn't even try. He wanted to take me back, and I was so relieved to find this friend, who I had abandoned, yet he was not worried about the wrong that I could still do him.

I returned to the Folies along with Lassagne, a beloved, popular actor. Obviously, he had talent, and he knew it. He always talked about opening a school and giving lessons and advice to Bouffe, Arnal, Odry. He never helped me with my acting. He took advantage of my embarrassment onstage to make me into a farce. It made his role that much greater. I never had a clever comeback, and I didn't know what I should do. To get a reaction from the audience, he would have booed his best friend.

Everyone knew him, and they kept their distance. Few people liked him. Often, M. Mouriez spoke to him harshly, and Mme. Odry begged him to stop what she called his "stunts" or he'd have to pay for it.

Among the actresses was Angélina Legros. She'd

been there for fifteen or sixteen years and was too distinctive to play many roles. She saw a rival in every other actress, and she did not handle it well. I debuted in one of her roles. I needed to make friends in the theater, and I had the naïvete to count on her. I quickly gave up on that illusion.

I knocked on other doors. I went to see Dinah, a short, pretty brunette with a babyish face. It didn't take me long to find her faults. She hadn't grown out of behaving childishly. I went to see Duplessis; that came to nothing at all. Only the woman in the neighboring dressing room, Frenex, remained. She was an extraordinary creature—short, so thin you could count her ribs, strawberry-blonde hair, a petite nose, teeth that looked like she'd bought them, a wide mouth, and pale lashes and brows. All this was painted in black, white, and red to make it passable. She was energetic, she was tiny, she was a good actress, and she was a coquette. A new friend was an achievement, and she welcomed me warmly. This lasted for several days.

She was unlucky in love, and I felt the backlash of her bad mood. I was sympathetic and followed her along the hall to Léontine's dressing room. Léontine clearly saw that this was a huge heartbreak; however, it made her forgive a little silliness. She no longer saw very well, and she was irritated that no one wanted to do what was necessary to play young girls. She had a good heart. M. Dennery cast her well as ChonChon when he made *The Grace of God*.

The Folies was not like other theaters. There was no green room for actors, and the wings were so small that you had to wait for your entrance in your dressing room. These rooms were as large and well lit as being inside a closed trunk. You'd die of boredom in there. That's why I went to visit all these women. At first it wasn't easy; there had been an announcement that I had been hired and was going to debut at the Folies.

"It's undignified to bring in Mogador as our colleague! What will that do the reputations of the other actresses at the Folies?"

If a dog bite makes you mad, the rudeness thrown at you from all sides, often without motive and always without reason, could very well make you a little rude.

Only one of my colleagues gave me advice that was any good, Mme. Odry. As for the men, that was another thing entirely. Hensey, Coutard, Boisselot, Hoster—all were charming to me and fought for the pleasure of giving me their opinions. I really did need them, and I followed their advice in order to improve.

35

OR WILL PRIDE BE ALLOWED TO FESTER?

RICHARD HAD BEEN MAKING A serious run at Mlle. Alice Ozy, but he quit that immediately. She was informed of the reason for his sudden coldness: me. Without my knowing, she set her sights on me.

One day I had Richard and one of his friends, Count B…, to dinner.

"By the way," the count said after dinner, "are you coming to the ball at Ozy's tomorrow? I'd be happy if you did. I'm afraid I won't know anyone there."

"You should go with Céleste," Richard said.

"Not only that," said his friend happily, "I'm going to ask for an invitation. It's right next door; I'll be back in five minutes."

It actually took him a quarter of an hour. I don't know what kind of premonition came over me, but I went into my bedroom and listened at the door.

"Well?" said Richard.

"Well! My friend, you didn't tell me that you had a delicate situation with her. Ozy refused me at once, and then she took it back, saying, 'I would like it very much if Richard came, but cannot allow Mlle. Mogador to come. That girl will never set foot in my house. The horror! Who do you think I am?'"

"Keep it to yourself," said Richard. "Don't say anything in front of Céleste."

I went back into the dining room without letting on that I knew anything. My self-esteem was working hard. I promised myself that the arrogant Ozy would welcome me within the week. This seemed easy enough to me. I remembered that Victorine knew her, so I went to talk to her. Victorine scolded me for being in town for so long without coming to see her.

"My dear, I deserve more of your scolding than you know. I only came today to ask a favor. But don't wait around for me in any case; the theater takes up all my time."

"I know that," she said, laughing. "I saw you perform a few days ago. You're not good."

"I was worried you'd say that."

"How did you get it into your head to act?"

"That's how irritated I was with Robert."

"Then it's a self-inflicted wound?"

"Oui, but I didn't come see you to talk about that. Imagine, my poor friend, that yesterday I was greatly insulted. An invitation from Mlle. Ozy was requested, but she refused in terms that hurt me. I want to meet her, I want to be seen with her. Can you help?"

"Non, I don't see her anymore. I'm surprised at her disdain; her talent's much the same as yours. As for your name, Mogador, you could do as she did and change it. It's nice, Alice Ozy, but that's not her name."

"Oh! Do you think you know what it is?"

"I don't think, I'm sure. It would seem to me that she should receive you as an equal. Oh! My word, she's staying at this very moment with Rose Pompon. You must know Rose Pompon!"

"Oui, I'll go to her place if I have to, but Mlle. Ozy will receive me in her home. Adieu, my dear friend, or see you again soon. I have business to take care of, and I only have a week to get it done."

"You have more time than it will take."

I arrived at Rose Pompon's place. She had dressed in every color to greet me. She had a piano teacher there who was paid to fawn over and compliment Mlle. Ozy. I understood that this teacher could help my cause. I asked her to come see me the next morning. She said that she could not come later than ten o'clock, as she had lessons at eleven with Mlle. Alice.

She arrived the next morning. She was a youngish forty. She began by telling me lots of terrible things about Ozy, even as she was dressed from head to toe in things she'd gotten through Ozy's generosity. I hadn't asked her to come over to inflict her ingratitude on me.

I broached the subject I did have in mind.

"Imagine, madame, that I have an urgent need to meet with Mlle. Ozy. I've heard she is a charming person. I know that this is quite difficult, but curiosity knows no bounds! Her apartment, they say, is sumptuous."

"And you would like to see it," she said, seeming protective.

"I admit, that's why I went to see Pompon. But I wasn't sure of where she stood with Ozy, so I didn't want to ask her for anything."

"And you were right! Mlle. Alice has gotten ideas about this Pompon, that she's a liar, she promises everything and delivers nothing. I'm going to tell Ozy that you find her lovely, that you speak only of her, of her luxurious life. Send her flowers, and within two days she'll ask if you'd like to come for a visit."

It worked. Ozy told me, via the piano teacher, that I'd been mistaken about how she felt about me. She had received a magnificent bouquet of flowers from me, and she asked me to come see the effect they had on her salon.

I hadn't begged or pleaded. She was charming, and she asked me to come back again as soon as possible. The next day, she sent word to ask if I wanted to dine at her fireside with her. My response was accompanied by another massive bouquet. She gave me a complete course in philosophy. She spoke of the Bible, of the grandeur and decadence of the Romans, and of their simple, modest taste. She repeated that she herself was a good person so often than I became convinced of it.

I received an invitation to her ball. What a perfect occasion to wear my emerald jewels!

I arrived first, because she had suggested that I should come early. Her apartment was literally overflowing with flowers and lights. It was the most beautiful thing I'd ever seen. She had exquisite taste.

People began to arrive. Ozy was dressed simply, which on her was spectacular, because she was so well put together.

Two women came into the salon, and she welcomed them. When she came back to stand next to me, I asked,

"Who are those two?"

"Mesdemoiselles Ber…"

"They're sisters?"

"Non, mother and daughter."

The daughter was thin as a rail and dressed like a child, with a wide ribbon sash. She carried a book and was about to scuttle into a small side room, saying that if she had known there would be such awful company, she wouldn't have come.

The awful company was me. Ozy shrugged and only became friendlier toward me. Some of the women received me kindly. Many were disdainful and haughty. I was not rude, but I took the hint to remember how I was treated.

Among all the women who were in the salon, one interested me more than the others. She was pretty as love, and she seemed friendly. I followed her with my eyes. I felt as if I liked her already; she had an irresistible charm. This was the little Page. I didn't dare speak to her, and Ozy refused to introduce her to me.

36

My Carriage

ALL OF THESE THINGS HELPED me pass the time for a month. The memory of Robert came to mind pretty often, and I'd hide myself away to cry.

One day Richard came to see me. He was ashen.

"What's happened, my friend?"

"Are you expecting any visitors today?"

"Non, why?"

"Okay," he said to me, "you're going to think I'm crazy. Don't lie. Have you seen him?"

"Who are you talking about?"

"Who? Your Robert, who I saw this morning. He is in Paris. Don't play dumb, you know this."

I couldn't answer. My legs felt weak. I am sure I became pale as death.

Richard took me by the arm and said, as he held me up, "It's obvious you still love him. You're shaking."

"I never said I didn't love him. I said that I wouldn't go to his house anymore."

"And I told you that you would sacrifice me the very next day, if it made you happy. I am the most miserable man alive!" He fell into a chair and dissolved into tears.

I didn't have the courage to say a word of consolation because I was as badly off as he was. Robert's distance and isolation were my strength. The idea of him being in Paris, maybe with another woman, tortured me. I only heard my own anguish; poor Richard was forgotten.

"Look," I said to him at last, "don't be a child and drain me of my little bit of resolve. I won't see him, and you know I would never make an effort to meet with him. He's already forgotten about me. Why tell me you saw him? I'm going to ignore the fact that he's here."

"I told you, Céleste, because he was coming from here. I thought he was leaving your place. I thought that he would retrace his steps and see me come inside."

Oh! The egotism of a great passion! Nature is cruel, and the heart is without pity for the suffering of others when it's nursing its own wounds!

I looked at Richard—this good, devoted man—with fury. I wanted him as far away from me as possible. In only a few moments, it was no longer possible for me to bear this pain. I needed to be absolutely alone.

"Hang on, Richard. Go home. I'll come see you tomorrow."

"You're sending me away."

"Non, my friend, I am begging you to leave me alone. I'm in pain."

He tossed a disapproving look at me, which was only

too fair. But I wasn't up for hearing it. It made me tired. I repeated my request as an order. I was devastated, and I didn't take care with my words. I was as upset as he was.

Robert was in Paris and had tried to see me! I didn't leave him with even the memory of friendship, so why? What did I do to him? Twenty times I'd had the idea of putting on my hat and going running through the streets until I ran into him by chance.

My maid, who had just come up, brought me a letter. It was from Robert:

> *I'm going to spend several days in Paris. If your work at the theater doesn't take too much of your time, come hold my hand. I'm staying on rue Royale, and you should come to dinner. If you cannot accept, come for just five minutes anyway. I have to speak to you.*

I took a small carriage and got myself to his place. It was maybe weak of me, but could passion inspire anything else?

His apartment was on the mezzanine, and I saw his face at the window behind a curtain. He was expecting me.

"To see a woman of your elegance getting out of such a small carriage," he said as he greeted me, "your lover is not generous. I would have you driven about in something much finer."

I looked at him in astonishment. "If that's what you wrote to tell me, don't bother. Even if I'm given little, I ask nothing from you." I moved toward the door.

He called after me, "You're in a bad mood. Forgive me, and let's make peace. I love you enough to not lose sight of where your interests lie. I know that you're back in the theater. It's a pedestal, and you as a woman should find some success. Men are stupid enough to watch all these performers. In the end, if this works for you, then it's for the best. I understand now why you were so anxious to leave me. Have you had brilliant affairs? Oh, don't worry. You can tell me as a friend. I want to help. A girl like you can't go out on foot; the police would arrest you. I'm going to give you a carriage as a gift."

He walked over to me. His eyes were serious, and his lips pressed into a line. He scared me, and I stepped back. I thought he'd gone mad.

He went on. "You can see that I have something to tell you. I have to tell you that you only inspire disgust. So how do you fascinate me? It's magic, right? An upstanding man could not love a creature like you. I was crazy when I caged you within my forefathers' chateau. For you, I forgot about the rules of decorum. What did you give me in exchange? A used-up body and a vile soul. You were an ingrate and low class. You didn't respect for one single day the thought of the man who had done so much for you. That's what I wanted to tell you. You can go repeat it to M. Richard, who is surely waiting for you downstairs."

He unlatched the door to let me out.

Blood raced to my head, and I went blind. I felt myself fall backward. When I came to, I felt the blood beating violently in my heart and veins. Anger overcame me. I was furious.

I walked toward him and loomed over him. "You had me come here to hurt me, and with what right, exactly? The right of a coward to do terrible things, the right to accuse others of doing you wrong in order to excuse yourself in your own eyes. Did I ask anything of you?

Did I go looking for you for some kind of closure? Did I lead you to all these foolish expenses? Did I plant your whims? You should be ashamed for what you've said to me. I never hid anything from you; I am in the books as a courtesan. It would have been kind of you to help me leave this position before taking me to your house. If I hadn't confided this terrible secret to you myself, you would have made me cry until my tears turned to blood. But I can look you in the eye with nothing to blame myself for. You took up with me, left me, took me back, and left. You no longer wanted me, and another man loved me. Is that such a crime? Come on! You threw me at the door, and another gathered me up. If you could drown the women you've lived with, that would be more convenient, isn't that true, monsieur le comte? What do you want? Justice isn't always fair."

I laughed nervously, which made the wound even worse, and left at a run, gasping. In the carriage, I sobbed.

I hurried to Richard's to tell him everything that had happened. He was kind to me and gently chided me for going there in the first place.

I went back home consumed by fever. It was too much. Robert again asked for me; surely he regretted the way he treated me, because he knew me. He must have understood all the despair in my heart. I refused to see him.

He came with his valet. He closed the door to the salon and came to sit beside me.

I got up and opened my armoire. I took out all the jewelry he'd given me and said, "Only one thing could bring you here, monsieur, the wish to see what you'd given me. I would give it back to you, but since I don't want you giving it to someone else as soon as you walk out the door, I'll destroy it." I lifted the jewelry box above my head and threw it across the room as hard as I could.

The box opened and diamonds, emeralds, and pearls rolled everywhere.

"You're mad," he said, toeing the box.

"Yes, sure, I'm mad with rage. I hate you. I will get revenge on you and all of high society if I can. Go on, I don't need any more from you. Get out. Just get out. You can see that I'm not about to cry."

After he left, I gratefully sank into an easy chair. I felt myself crash. I was frighteningly angry—dangerously, even. I'd lost my sanity. When the reaction came at last, I did cry. Then I was sick for several days.

The next day, Robert called on me, gave me a glass of water, and said, "Don't let my presence upset you, Céleste. I was wrong, and I came to ask your forgiveness. What do you want? Yesterday when I came, I hastened to see you because I only made this trip to make up with you. I ran into M. Richard outside. He was coming here, which made me lose my head. When I had you over, I was still under this influence."

He tried to take my hand. I pulled it away. Exalted by my anger, I yelled, "My God! Let me just die! I will kill myself to get away from you, Robert, and from a world that has made me pay dearly for my fall from grace. Cursed is the day I stepped foot onto this road that looks like flowers and dreams and is in fact shadows. Then when you see the light, you can see all the way to the bottom of the abyss. You can see the snakes that follow you and are fascinated by your broken youth. Go, leave. I'm depressed."

Robert got to his knees and used soothing words to try to calm the delirium I'd fallen into. When I came around, I'd mostly forgotten what had happened.

His eyes brimming with tears, he said, "Forgive me. I promise you, I'll never do it again."

"I want to forgive you, Robert, but I can't promise to forget."

I spent the entire next day in bed. He didn't leave my side even once.

I received a letter from Richard:

I waited for you all day. Do you know what it's like to wait for someone you love the way that I love you? Rather than lose you completely, I'll resign myself to the entire situation, but I want to see you, only for five minutes. Céleste, I loved you because I thought you had a good heart, so have mercy on me. If I can't see you tomorrow, I'll take it badly. I know perfectly well that you don't love me like him, but I have a claim to your friendship. You can't reduce me to despair when I would give my life to spare you a single tear. I want to believe that you are not acting freely. I want to be brave enough to wait until tomorrow.
Richard

He was right, and his request was so sweet that it was impossible to push aside. However, I had an aversion to lying, to tricks. It was maybe the only benefit of the sad life I led: the power to tell the truth, no matter how hard it might be. The sidestepping I had to do made me hesitate, and I said to Robert, "My friend, I'm going to the theater. They'll be waiting for me."

Since our fight, he had been tender and sweet. You have no idea.

"Go," he said. "I'll wait for you here."

Once I got to the boulevard, I turned to look at my window. He was there, and he followed me with his eyes for as long as he could see me.

When I arrived at Richard's, he had a large box next to him. He had written several letters, and he was still writing when I came in.

"Ah! It's you," he said as he stood. He was so pale I thought he must be in pain. "Thank you for coming. It would be awful if I died without seeing you."

"Die!" I said, taking his hands and making him sit down beside me. "Die! You're so young, so beautiful, so happy! Don't ever say this word."

"Why not," he said, "when it's the only way to regain my lost sense of calm? Look, I've spent all night writing." He pointed out the letters that I'd already seen. Then he opened the box, took out one of the pistols inside, and showed me it was loaded. "I'm only afraid of one thing," he said. "That I'll miss."

People with the gentlest personalities often experience the most violent depressions. I did not doubt for an instant that what he said was true and that his mind was made up.

I ran to his side. "Put the pistol back, Richard. You're scaring me."

"You're wrong, Céleste, about death. It's a good thing for me! I love you like a madman. That's not real love; that's a hallucination. You can't love me, so you can see then that I have to die. Who will miss me? My father was poisoned in Maurice when I was twelve. My mother died when I was fifteen. No one will shed a tear for me. I wanted to protect you from need. I leave you all that I have. When you are down, think of me. No one will ever love you like I love you."

As he said all this, he fiddled with the pistol in his hands. I heard a sound—he had cocked it. I threw myself onto him and tried to wrestle the pistol away from him. In the struggle, there was a second where the barrel was turned toward my face.

"Let go of me," he said. "Protect yourself."

"Non," I answered, and I doubled down on my efforts. "Kill me if you want, it's no great loss. But I beg you, don't do this to yourself."

He pulled away, and the shot went of high and to the side. The bullet punctured my portrait. We quickly went into the next room, and he signaled for me to not say anything. I leaned against the desk.

His butler came in, very upset. "Pardon me, monsieur, for disturbing you, but I heard a gunshot—"

"It's nothing," said Richard. "I was playing with my pistol, and the trigger is so sensitive that it went off."

When the butler had left, Richard looked at my portrait on the wall. The bullet had gone through its forehead. Turning back to me, he said, "Look, since you don't want me to kill myself, what can you do to help me want to go on living?"

"I could assure you, Richard, that I am your most devoted friend. If I had met you sooner, how I would have loved you! But what do you want? Wait a little while. Everything will be different in a few days. Maybe we could go out together then? We'll take a big trip, if you want. But don't lose hope. I will come see you."

"You promise, Céleste?"

"Yes, if you'll be all right."

"I promise I will. When will you come back?"

"Day after tomorrow."

I returned to my place entirely drained after this scene. Robert looked me in the eyes. He was trying to see into my soul.

Several days passed. Robert knew me too well to not see the change at work inside me. Certainly I loved him more than anyone, but I could not break Richard's heart. He threatened me with the wildest extremes. Being in this position was killing me and making me depressed and cold. Robert noticed, and I didn't even dare hold his hand. A shadow fell between him and me.

He said to me one morning, "I'm leaving the city this evening, which should make you happy. Your freedom is so important to you! I wanted to give you a gift before I go, but it's not ready. You'll receive it tomorrow."

"But my friend, I don't need anything. You're wrong to spend anything on me, whatever it may be."

"If, my dear child, your theater is far from here, you'll need a carriage. I want you to be both happy and elegant. Me, I'm a pathetic companion. You'll have more fun when I'm not there. I want to let you enjoy your life."

The whole situation hit me so hard that for the first time, I accepted the news of his departure for the country without feeling bad. Plus, I have to confess, that at the first mention of the carriage, my imagination ran riot. Robert left that night.

I spent the whole next day watching out the window. At four o'clock, I saw a delicious little coupe stop at my door. A man jumped out of his seat with a paper in his hand. I ran down like an arrow shot from a bow. They asked for me. It was indeed my carriage, and it was hitched to a pretty bay horse. The harness was marked with my monogram. On the door panel, a small shield surrounded my initials with the motto "Forget me not" in English. The coupe was painted bright blue, and the interior was upholstered in the same color. I walked around it ten times. I went in one side and got out the other. I touched the ivory decorations, and I opened and closed the windows. I looked at passersby in triumph. In my head, I said to them, *Hey! What do you think?* My joy was brought up short when I realized I couldn't keep it all up in my room. Where was I going to put a horse and carriage?

Everything had been taken care of. Robert had rented a stable and carriage house on rue Rougemont. The driver, dressed in the English fashion, had received orders to come here at four o'clock, the hour of the promenade on the boulevard. I quickly went upstairs to get dressed. I was so flustered, I put on a green dress, a red shawl, and a yellow hat. I looked like a parrot. The two hours of the promenade seemed so short. Everyone said "Oh!" and "Ah!" when they saw me. I was delighted. If anyone who saw me could read my lips, I would have told them, "It's mine, not a rental."

Having soaked up all the attention on the street, I went to my building. At the corner of boulevard de Madeleine, I noticed Richard. Oh, the wretched frivolousness of a woman enchanted by her new toy! My first excursion was one of pride.

I was happy for him to see me. I waved to him and called out. My carriage didn't seem to make him as happy as it made me. He walked away grumpily.

Back at my house, I dressed in less garish clothing and resigned myself to going, *on foot*, to visit Richard.

Instead of complimenting me on my beautiful horse and carriage, he said coldly, "How will you pay the rent to keep them?"

I rubbed my forehead and didn't answer. He was right; this was a massive expense. But since I wanted to be happy without worrying for once, I frowned and said, "I'm leaving tomorrow for Giscars. I'm going to see my little goddaughter."

37

LONDON

I ARRIVED AT THE HOME of the wet nurse, without whom my goddaughter would not have survived. I was let into the house and found a poor little creature alone in a crib, so pale, so weak, that she seemed on the brink of death. I noticed that she was wearing the things I had bought for her. I picked up the child, and her head lolled to the side. The nurse was out at the shops. She came back half an hour later.

I stepped up to her and said in her face, "Are you insane to leave an infant alone? You haven't taken care of her. She's sick. That wasn't the deal. I pay you more than I should. If anything happens to her, watch your back. The poor thing only wants to live."

This woman gave me the worst excuses. We dressed the baby, who started smiling at me. I couldn't leave until the evening train, so I spent the entire day there.

The husband came in not long after his wife. He seemed at least as embarrassed as she was. It seemed as if they were hiding something from me. The little one began to cry, and the nurse rocked her.

"She must be hungry," I said.

"My God, madame," the husband said, "that's what's been bothering us ever since you arrived. We haven't dared to tell you, but the child has been weaned because my wife is pregnant."

"Oh, for the love," I cried as I seemed to leave my body. "Now the state of this poor angel makes sense. You have poisoned her with your bad milk. And in order to not lose the money I send you, you're going to end up killing her, you stupid shits! That's how so many mothers end up bereft: You take more than their life, their child. It's too horrible to even consider. I don't know what is keeping me from having you arrested, because this child has a week to live. Quick, go get a doctor."

After a few minutes, a doctor arrived. I showed him the baby.

"Poor little thing, she's suffered. She's so frail. They're all the same: they wean them at three or four months, and they give them cabbage soup with potatoes, same as the pigs. They all have tumors after two weeks of it. This one, too, but maybe you can save her if you take care of her."

I wanted to beat this fucking woman who had so brazenly lied to me. I picked up my precious little girl and took her back to Paris on the train: a suitcase on my left, a bottle to my right, and my goddaughter on my knees.

I admit that I was a little embarrassed. I kept her

at my place for three days, and after finding her a good foster home, I occupied myself with my lovely carriage.

Robert came to Paris. My secret life began again, and I was afraid he would make up his mind.

I went to Richard's and told him, "My dear friend, I came to ask for proof of your affection. Do you love me enough to make a sacrifice?"

"Do you doubt it?"

"I don't doubt it, but I would be more positive if you did what I'm going to ask of you."

"What's bothering you?"

"My ability to relax. Robert is in town. I can see that this makes you furious. I have to hide, to be suspicious of everyone who goes by. I cannot get used to this constraint. What always lures Robert is your presence, so leave town. Go on a little vacation. You told me that you have business in Brussels. If Robert leaves me—and it cannot happen soon enough—I'll come find you."

"I'm an inconvenience, so you want to get rid of me?"

"Non, my friend, but I can't live like this. Go. I'll write to you every day. If you stay in town, I can't see you anyway."

After making a thousand objections, he promised to leave the next day. I took him at his word and thanked him with all my heart.

Robert was back in his apartment on rue Royale, and his moods were swinging wildly. One day he was so sweet to me, another he harassed me, then he'd ask my forgiveness and insult me all over again. Every time we made up, he gave me the most magnificent gifts. He had given me the pretty little carriage, all in blue, which belonged to him but had my name on it. He'd also given me the two beautiful black horses that I had seen drawing his phaeton the first day he'd come to see me on rue Geoffrey-Marie.

I had one of the most beautiful teams of horses on the Champs-Élysées, and I was dripping with jewels, cashmere, and lace. But I was sobbing behind my veil.

I could never say how he made me suffer. He went from insult to adoration in a snap. My heart was stormy, my life hellish. I was not yet at the point where I could tell myself, A day will come where I will win over him, where I will be able to make plans for my own happiness. I lived without a goal, without hope. Short bursts of joy, long stretches of boredom, and unending despair: That was my life.

Robert was incapable of letting me go to let me be happy. He became insane with rage when realized he couldn't remove me from his heart. Sometimes, after a dinner where a fit of rage rather than the wine worked him up, he thought he was strong enough to break this chain that was making each day worse. Then the spell would fall away, and he would grovel at my feet, more humble and in love than ever. When Richard was in Paris, it would send Robert into a fury. When Richard was out of town, since Robert had nothing more to fear, he was calmer. But he was still a loose cannon, so I won nothing in the end. Luckily, an opportunity came up that meant we would see each other less often, and I eagerly seized it.

I was asked to perform a new piece at the theater called *Les Martyrs du Carnaval*. I said to myself, *If he sees me less, Robert will love me much more. He'll be nicer.* But in fact it made things worse. The theater exasperated him because I danced in every scene. I often came to work with red eyes. The poor chorus girls who only made twenty-five francs a week were better off than me.

When Richard was out of town, Robert thought it was good for my heart. When he was in Paris, I hardly even noticed. Robert had convinced me that even a smile was too much attention to pay to Richard. When he wasn't in town anymore, my thoughts gladly turned to the familiarity of Richard. This was not love, it was a crush. The memory of him benefited from my reaction to Robert's violence. Plus, Richard wrote me the kindest, most affectionate letters from Brussels. Far be it from me to resist a plea so sweet!

Dear Céleste,
You ordered me to leave because your sanity depended on it, and I left. I am at pains to restrain my tears. You, on the other hand, have a laughing face and seem happy. When I was alone in the train car, I cried like a baby! When I think of where I stand with you, my heart is heavy. I love you, and you don't love me. I am so unlucky in love! You make others happy with no mercy for me. You never asked what would happen to me when I was alone with my despair. Non, this means nothing to you. I don't think you know even now how much I love you. I don't even know myself! As long as we're happy, we're lucky. It's hard to know at what cost. But when we lose it, there aren't enough tears to cry for what's been lost. If this separation lasts any longer, I won't survive. I wish I

knew how to stop being a martyr to this rage that burns and chokes me. Oui, Céleste, I would die for you, but as I died I would only have words of love and adoration in my mouth. That would leave you happier with your other lovers. Would you still be unmoved? Would you not then have a word of consolation for me? I have a raging fever. I've been given quinine. It doesn't do anything. Think of me and I'll get well! I close my eyes and imagine myself being near you. I'm very happy then, but it's only a flash that vanishes as quickly as it came. What did I do to be loved by you? Nothing, absolutely nothing, because my insane passion for you does not count—passion that I very much feel will ruin my life and will only end when I do. This letter is going to bore you. It holds all that it can hold—the expression of my love. You remain the same, always so cold, so indifferent. Why don't you just lie to me? It would be kinder to lead me on. It's so easy to believe those lies when you're miserable. When someone like me loves the way I love you, there should be at least a little pity for the one who suffers. I know your heart better than you. You think you hate this man, but you love him more than ever.

I received a letter from you. You granted me a freedom that I find detestable. You took away all hope of getting back together. Don't worry; I don't blame you. Besides, you're not mine, and my love for you is too great to kiss the hand that slaps me. You can break my heart, but you'll never kill my love. I need to distract myself. Maybe gambling will let me forget for a moment! A word from you, a sign, and I would be at your feet. I will always wait for you.

    Richard

This letter was too kind. Poor Richard! I blamed myself for making him miserable. But he was young, and I hoped his being out of the city would help him forget.

At the same time that *Les Martyrs du Carnaval* was playing at the Folies, there was also a piece called *Blanche et Blanchette*. In the role of the lover was a new young, thin, dark-haired boy—handsome, with a bright complexion. He was called Alexis Didier. At first I didn't take any notice of him, but people told the most extraordinary stories about him that I began to pay more attention. I looked for reasons to talk to him, to hear him. Keep mind that I didn't believe in magnetism, and I laughed in the faces of fortune tellers.

Didier is the clairvoyant sleepwalker that M. Dumas studied for so long. There were séances at his house. Everyone went, and by the time they left, they were convinced it was real! I was invited to one, but I turned it down because I did not believe in sleepwalking as divination at all. People told Didier I was a complete skeptic. He came up to talk to me, as we often had a reason to chat. When his small talk went on for more than ten minutes, I became tired and numb. When he took my hand, it was an effort to pull it away.

"Go on, Didier. They'll say that you're flirting with me."

He answered without taking his eyes from mine. "Let them talk!"

"Non, I can't." I escaped, but not for long. After I'd mingled for a while, I came back to him.

He began to laugh and said, "You see, you came looking for me!"

I said I had and stood rooted to the spot. It was all so stupid. I promised myself that the next day, as soon as my scene was over, I'd quit the theater because everyone would be laughing at me. Surely they would think I was in love with Didier. I was not at all into him.

My play went on before his, so he came to the theater after I did. I told people in my dressing room, "Wait! Didier has arrived!"

"Non," they answered, "his dressing room door is closed."

"I tell you, he's here, I heard him." In truth, he was in the foyer of the theater.

⁂

One evening, at the theater, I received a note. It was from Richard.

I must see you tomorrow. Come to my place, or I'll come to yours!

His return to the city no longer bothered me, but I couldn't let him come to my apartment. I went to see him.

He had changed. He looked exhausted. He asked me to sit and said, "I have come back, though you didn't ask me to. It didn't even occur to you. But I couldn't live without you. Listen well, Céleste. You're going to see just how much this love has taken hold of my life. I've thought about it, and here's what I have to offer you: a happy future and an honest life, which will help you move on from a past I will never bring up. I will give you forty thousand francs. We will leave immediately for England, where I will be able to marry you because I have English citizenship and don't have parents. Hear me out.

You can't say no, because you have treated me badly. You should make it up to me by making this sacrifice. I didn't go looking for you at that ball; you came to me! I didn't seek you out, you flirted with me. It's a gamble that has cost me dearly and that will end my life if you say no."

I didn't know how to answer. What he said was true. I hid my face in my hands to cry.

"I can't accept your proposal. It's crazy; you haven't thought it through."

"Excuse me," he said, "but I've thought about it so well and for so long that you must answer now."

"But that's impossible!"

He stood up, looking insane. I was afraid. I pulled him close and said, "Look, my friend, be reasonable. I was so far from expecting what you've said that I'm stunned. Give me time to think. Besides, are you sure that this can be taken care of in London? Go make sure, take two or three days. I'll write to tell you when to come back to find me."

"You're lying, Céleste. You won't write to me."

"I promise that I will write."

"I have to believe you. I'll leave tonight."

He was content, but I myself became depressed. I would write to him, but only to make him give up this insane idea.

A few days later, I was having lunch at Robert's on rue Royale, along with one of his friends. In the middle of the meal, Robert tried to start a fight with me, as usual. It started as nothing and—again, as usual—it finished in a raging storm.

"For the last time," I said to him, "are you blaming me?"

"I do blame you—for having poisoned my heart and made me blush to have feelings for the famous Mogador! I hate you because…I hate you, in the end, because I love you."

He went into his bedroom, leaving me with his friend.

"He's nuts!" said his friend.

"Oui, and cruel, so it would be better to leave than to live like this. But that's exactly the offer I turned down for his sake." And I told him of Richard's proposal.

"If that's true," he said to me doubtfully, "it was a mistake to say no, for Robert's sake and your own, because it would ruin him. He has to get married."

"You very well know that he's tried a hundred times, and it always falls apart."

"Because he knows you're there, so he never takes marriage seriously. He wouldn't keep failing at marriage arrangements if he wanted to go through with it, with his name, his reputation, his wealth. If you were out of town, and he no longer had any hope, you'd see that he'd do it."

Robert came back in, apologized for his bad mood, and tried to make me forget about it. But once my eyes were brimming with tears, those tears dried slowly.

I received a letter from Richard. Despite what I had written to him, he repeated the same proposal and begged me to accept.

This offer was too serious to not consider. He wasn't

only advocating for his own happiness, but also mine!

The theater bored me. To be an actor requires a routine life. It's difficult to be happy onstage, to sing, to dance, to make others laugh, when your heart is sad.

Didier continued to persuade me out of my disbelief by exercising a magnetic influence over me that made me tired! Sometimes I got annoyed, and he would say to me, laughing, "Are you starting to believe?" I would answer, "Non!" in order to not give in. But I couldn't deny that he'd done something supernatural to me. He somehow increased his influence, and I followed his every step around the theater. I almost always knew where he was without seeing him. This concerned me *and* irritated me. Eventually I realized that it was going on too long.

One day when Robert had invited Montji to dinner, he picked a fight with me again. I'd never been a patient person—that day, even less so. The fight became so terrible that my secret escaped me.

"My dear friend, do you think I need you? Do think that when I leave here, I won't find a friend to take my hand on the other side of your door? But I wouldn't have anyplace to go, I wouldn't know where to eat, that I wouldn't stay with you, if you keep treating me like a courtesan! If you don't love me anymore, or if you're so angry because you love me too much, it's not my fault. You don't have any right to make my life so hard! Why, when you came back to Paris, did you seek me out? Your personality is the badminton racket, and my happiness is the birdie. I don't want to live like this anymore. Listen to what I'm telling you: I have to write Richard tomorrow with my decision. Your response right now is going to determine mine tomorrow. I still love you, and the proof is that I'm here. I've been offered marriage and forty thousand francs immediately if I will leave you. I never intended to tell you, but before I make up my mind, I want you to give me your word of honor that you'll no longer treat me the way you have been for some time now. This life is hell! It would be better for us to break up for good."

"Bravo!" he said with a burst of laughter. "The scene was well acted, the climax original. But, my dear child, I'm not your gullible audience. Who gives you such good acting lessons? Oh, someone wants to marry you! You've been offered money to leave me, and you came to tell me so that I'll match the price to keep you. Fine! Here's my answer: If what you say is true, I say you accept his offer. First, my intention was never to keep you around for the long term, and second, I had no idea you were sacrificing so much to be with me! Not that I believe this offer is real."

To be suspected of a double-crossing scheme seemed more odious to me than all the rest of it.

I left in exasperation, vowing to never return and finally deciding to leave town. I went to the theater and begged M. Mouriez to let me have a few days off. He allowed it.

I went back to my place and found this letter from Robert:

When you love a woman as low-class as can be and are too weak to break up with her, you make yourself blind and dumb, and that's what I should have done. But I can't do what God himself wouldn't be able to do. The heart of a girl like you is like a whorehouse. The passing respectable man who wanders in by accident finds all the usual amenities of a normal hotel. When a good feeling wells up

in his heart, evil passions, like the mistress of the whorehouse, very quickly chase the feeling away. You say that I didn't love you, but the love I had for you is my only excuse. If I hadn't loved you, I would be the lowest of the low. Your pretense of love began with a kiss and ended with a bill. I'm not rich enough. You're free.
Robert

I picked up a pen to write to Richard. My maid came in to announce that he was here. Impatience had brought him. I let out a shout of joy. He asked for my answer.

I said, "When do we leave?"

"Tomorrow evening, if you want. You must get your mother's blessing, and I would like you to deposit the money before we depart." He placed a wallet I had given him as a present on my vanity.

"Non, I don't want the money. Maybe later. We'll see."

"I want you to deposit it before leaving Paris. It's not a huge fortune, but it will help you raise your little girl. In any case, these forty thousand francs are for you."

I was confused by such generosity. I might have refused it again when Robert's words came to mind: *Not that I believe this offer is real.* I took the wallet and, showing it to the Robert in my mind, I said to him, Now you see I wasn't lying.

❦

Everything was ready the next evening: mother's blessing given, money deposited. We embarked. I asked to have my letters forwarded.

I felt ill when we boarded the train. I tried in vain to

think only of the man who had done everything for me, who was going to give me his name. My rebel heart knew that it was traveling far from Robert. I was ashamed of myself. I had no willpower. I could steer my body, but not my heart.

Richard asked if I was happy. I didn't answer so I wouldn't have to lie.

Once we were underway, I had more freedom. I could cry.

We had a very bad crossing. Richard was so ill he was almost unconscious. Out of about three hundred passengers, two of us stood on the deck throughout the storm. I stood fast against a column. With my arms crossed, I watched the furious waves, which seemed to chase our ship in order to swamp it. I waited for them. I was ready to let myself be carried away.

When day broke, I learned that we had been in real danger. We were lost. The passengers didn't even look human, especially M. Eugène Crémiux, horse trader, who I recognized as being one of Robert's merchants. He was frighteningly seasick. I had noticed, at the fore of the ship, a tall gentleman who never stopped smoking his cigar, even during the gale. Richard had gone to talk to him, so I asked his name.

"That's the prince of Syracuse."

"That makes sense!" I said. "He has sea legs."

When we arrived in London, we rented a large suite, and I went for a walk. Even from this first outing, I was horrified by this city. The fog obscured the daylight and only parted to allow a black snow that stained my white hat and smeared across my face. I went back inside, furious. I wanted to wash myself with soap and water; I looked like a chimney sweep. That was how bad it was.

The mistress of the house, who was very friendly and spoke French, said, "Madame does not know London. You don't wear light colors outside in this season, and always wear a green gauze veil." I thanked her, promising myself that I would not follow her advice. I didn't have the fortitude to dress like the English.

I figured out that cold cream removed most of the dirt from my face. I only went out in a carriage from then on. I visited all the monuments. One thing surprised me: You had to pay at every door to enter and exit, hand over I don't know how many shillings to see some jewelry in a glass case. I told myself that if the French were like that, foreign visitors wouldn't have enough money to see everything. I found this ransom in bad taste. Since we had more beautiful things in my own country, I no longer bothered with these. I was depressed, and I was bored. Richard only knew one way to keep me occupied: He bought me everything I looked at. The salon of our apartment became a shop of dresses, lace, and jewels.

He had arranged everything for our marriage. The moment drew near, not without giving me anxiety. I doubted myself, my resolve. It was even worse after I'd been to the post office, where I found a letter from Robert. He'd bribed my maid, and despite my wishes she'd told him where I was and how he could write to me. I hid this letter, since Richard was waiting for me and I didn't dare read it in front of him. At last when he went out alone, I broke the seal, my heart pounding. Here's what Robert wrote:

If you're even still accepting letters from me, don't think that I'm hoping for a reconciliation between us. You saw me as weak because I had hope. But today, what can I believe in? I believed in love before the day you spurned me, but since then, I don't believe in anything. You remained within truth, pleasure, novelty, profit, and a guarantee for the future. Me, who only lived by my heart and my imagination, I tried to ruin... I had a false courage. You abandoned me. Now there is a barrier that I will never cross. With you, Céleste, I have only suffered! I suffered for the past, I suffer for the present, and I will suffer all my life. If you marry this man, it will be a huge mistake! Once the novelty has worn off, he will only have blame and bitterness. The head is everything for him; the heart is nothing. If my advice carries any weight with you, I would be happy to send as good luck all that I have endured since your departure. I didn't believe you'd go until I had material proof. I searched for a distraction and found none. I don't have the heart to keep looking. You are the only woman for me. I'm up against the impossible. Why would I want this for you? Didn't I give you everything a person could have? Will this man be more content with your kisses than I was? Will he be kinder? It's not possible! Once his imagination is satisfied, what's left? Nothing! I will get my revenge on him, because he will not suffer more than I suffer.

You punished me with letters and words inspired by your anger. It ripped you apart because you didn't know how to find all of the passion and hopelessness inside. The woman in love has no other way of proving her love than through devotion, self-sacrifice. She would want to be the last person on earth, to owe everything to the one she loves, and be proud of that. You were like that when you loved me. Now that you no longer do, I embarrass you. That's how it should be.

Forgive me for bothering you in the middle of your

happy day. If my letter finds you in a sad mood, you will surely immediately find consolation in the kiss that you give to or get from him.
   Adieu.
   Robert

After reading this, I wept. However, I was still happy. This letter proved he loved me.

Richard came in. I thought I might lose my mind. I had already started to make a plan to leave. I was not even thinking of him anymore.

The formalities required to make our marriage official were in place, the services bought and paid for.

Richard said to me, "Well, Céleste, today is the day you become my wife. It's the greatest proof of my love that I can give you. Make me happy, and I'll be grateful to be yours."

He had brought me to London with a complete wardrobe. I dressed myself mechanically. I didn't dare say a word. I didn't want to get married, and I didn't know how to make him understand that we were both going to our undoing.

I wore a pearl-gray dress with brocade, a black lace shawl, and a white hat.

"This outfit is half in mourning," I said. "It's horribly depressing!"

He affixed a gorgeous veil to my hat, one that had been made for the queen. He'd bought it the day before.

I let myself be led out, but when the carriage stopped, my wits and my life came back to me.

"Non, non," I said to the coachman. "Don't stop, keep going! Richard, tell him to pass by this door. I have to talk to you." I settled myself inside the carriage and held onto the cushion as if I was going to be dragged out by force.

Richard gave the order to return to our hotel. He didn't say a word the entire way back. I didn't dare raise my eyes to look at him. Back in our rooms, he showed me to an easy chair, took another chair for himself, and said, "All right, Céleste. What do you have to tell me?"

He said this so sweetly, and he looked at my so kindly, that I hardly knew how to answer. My half-lowered veil hid my blush. I trembled, and my teeth chattered.

"Tell me what you're thinking. You're not saying anything," he said. "I'll tell you, then. You've realized you're afraid of the vows you're about to take. You don't love me, and you don't have the courage to give your life entirely over to me. There's no blame in saying no; it's honesty. Another man has taken my name and dragged it through the dirt. I'm offering you a secure future, but you don't want it. You don't love me, and you will never love me. I'll kill my love for you, or it will kill me!"

He hid his face in his hands to cry. I threw myself at his knees, and I begged his forgiveness for the wrong I was doing him. "Richard, be disgusted with me, I'm not worthy of a love like yours. Send me away. I'm a bitch. But I'm miserable! It's not my fault. Have mercy on me, don't burden me with your disdain, I couldn't bear it. Oh! I'm suffocating! I can't see…I'm going to die."

I fainted.

When I came to, I was in an overstuffed chair. I'd been undressed. The mistress of the house had put me in a dressing gown. I was about to ask what had happened when Richard gestured that I should stay quiet.

When we were alone, he took my hand and said, "The air in London has made you ill, Céleste. We're leaving tomorrow." He sat for a few moments without speaking; then, looking at me angrily, he said, "How you love him, that man!"

The rest of our time in London passed in silence. We departed the next day with very different emotions in our hearts.

Back in Paris, he got out of the carriage at a hotel, cité Bergère, because he had sold our apartment while we were away.

Robert learned very quickly of my return. He wrote me many letters that I didn't answer. I didn't belong to myself. That knowledge made me want to stay with Richard. I didn't want to go out with him, to request a meeting that, I knew, would have terrible consequences.

I received a new letter from Robert.

I forgive you for all the wrongs you have done to me. When I told you that I love you, that I suffer, you didn't find in your heart even the echo of a memory! It's wrong, Céleste, to be ungrateful. You didn't forgive me my moment of indiscretion, you berated me for not loving you anymore. You're being a bit unfair on this point. The day you no longer loved me, you had enough mercy to hide it from me, to lie to me until you thought you'd paid enough for my love. Thank you, my child. Why not let my dream last a few more hours? It's so nice for me; if only you knew, as in a kiss, that I would give you love, tenderness, passion! These kisses come from the bottom of my heart. Do they not turn your heart a least a little in the direction of the fire that consumes me? Now you don't love me, you don't understand me. It's done, then. I'll no longer see you. I'm going to go away, far away! Why show my tears? I'd be laughed at, and everyone would feel sorry for you, that's all. Come back to me, I ask forgiveness for all that could have offended you, even if I didn't think anything of it. Come see me to at least say goodbye. I never meant to hurt you. Don't leave me like this. I love you. Come back, and you will have more than you could ever dream of! I can't live without you. Come, come—it's my heart that's calling to you. I am sick in bed. Will you refuse a small mercy to a man whose only crime is having loved you too much? Will you let him die without a kind word? Non, I know your heart. You will come. I'm waiting for you.

The next day, there were races at Champ-de-Mars. I readied my coach to go. When I got downstairs, I found my carriage full of roses. I thought this was a grand gesture from Richard, and I went off. I brought along a little note that I wanted to leave for Robert, saying:

You love me today because I am with someone else. If he was no longer around, you wouldn't lower yourself to pick me up off the ground. I warned you! Before choosing, my heart was tormented. You well know that I love you, and you humored me, teased me. I left you, and you wrote to me of being wounded. I bore it all without saying a word of blame. I have a huge heart. I'm leaving you, and I'm going to the races. I need to gamble with my luxury, my success! I've made three people miserable, but everyone there will admire me. I am at the pinnacle of these women I've despised. The horses, the carriage—with all this, there's no need for a heart. Life is a bridge that spans the soul. At the beginning, there was love; at the end, ambition and pride.

I took up with you first, but you pushed me away, and I left with another. That's your doing. All the blame that

you heaped on me, I'm throwing it back at you. My heart is not a whorehouse! I followed you to prove this to you, despite my being a courtesan.
  Céleste

I gave this letter to a messenger. I didn't think I was brave enough to deliver it myself.

38

The next day, at eleven a.m., the doctor who had taken care of me back at place de la Madeleine, the one Robert kept on retainer, asked to speak to me. He was shown into my parlor.

After a perfunctory greeting, he said, "As strange as it must seem to you, I have come here of my own accord. I've just left the house of M. le comte …. It was the fourth visit I've made since yesterday at six o'clock. I've treated him twice for a very violent illness—choking on his own blood, leading to delirium. His valet told me that during the night he asked twenty times for someone to find you, but no one dared. I came to ask you to go to him. He may only have an hour left. He is sorry, it's the greatest of his regrets. I don't know what your relationship to one another is, but I didn't wait to find out. I remembered that with only a word from me, he brought you to his house in the country when he realized that you were dangerously ill."

My heart stopped.

I didn't take the time to answer. I put on a shawl and a hat and I said to the doctor, "Let's go. I'm ready."

When I arrived at his house on rue Royale, I was terrified. The servants were running back and forth. Robert was in the middle of a serious crisis, so they asked that I not go in. They thought that seeing me might make him worse. I was hearing none of it and went into his room. He was changed. His cheeks were pale, his eyes bright as lamplight. I approached his bed, and he looked at me for two or three minutes. Then, as if coming out of a dream, he leaned out of his bed and grabbed me around the waist.

"Oh! It's you," he said. "Come closer so that I can see how the face of a woman who can cause such trouble is made. You have the kiss of a viper. It poisons! Ghouls drink blood, but you—you devour the heart, you rend it with your claws, and when your victim is in agony, you become real, not to carry him off to safety but to play out your masterpiece of destruction. Who brought you here? I must be in hell to see you. But I'm not dead; I still have enough strength to crush you like the snake you are!" He grabbed my wrist so hard it bruised.

I didn't dare say a word or make a move. He was out of his mind.

He started to laugh. "You're turning pale. You're scared. The charm has fallen away, and I see you as you are. By what magic did you seduce me, daughter of Satan? You filled my veins with fire, and now it's gone to my head."

He released me to bring both hands to his forehead. His shirt was stained with black blood. He had opened the wounds where he'd been bled by the doctor. I called out, and the doctor rebandaged his arms, then assured me this was a good sign.

Eventually Robert seemed to calm down. He said, as if seeing me for the first time, "Ah! There you are. I'm glad you came. I've been waiting for you for so long. I'm going to get up; I'm weak. You'll stay with me, right? I need to see you. Where have you been? It seems like I haven't seen you in so long."

"Oui," I said, "I'll stay, I won't leave you." I removed my shawl and hat. I took a seat at the head of his bed, not daring to breathe.

He spoke to me of this and that and then fell asleep.

As he was leaving, the doctor said to me, "Don't leave his side. He's been bled, and he could have a new episode. I'll come back early tomorrow. If anything happens, send for me."

Once I was alone with the silence and my patient, I thought about my situation, of Richard, who I was about to let down. But I couldn't abandon Robert at a time like this. I went over to the table where the writing supplies were and began a letter for Richard.

> *My friend, I am unworthy of your love. It is with bowed head that I beg your forgiveness for the hurt that I'm still causing you. Forget me—I'm an ingrate and not good enough for you. Louise, my maid, will return the money, which I cannot keep. Don't come looking for me. Leave town if you must, but forget about me.*
>
> *Robert is seriously ill. I am at his bedside, and I'm*

not leaving his room until he is out of danger. Don't think that I've been dragged into being a nurse and that I'm trying to excuse his behavior with a lie. I'm not being held prisoner, and the doors are unlocked. I'm staying because it seems like I should.

I met you too late, Richard, or else I would have loved you as you deserve to be loved. I believed, when I came here, that Robert was going to kill me. I'm sorry that he didn't. My life is a wound on the world. I make those I love suffer, and I am unhappy in the midst of it all.

Don't feel bad for me, my friend. Have mercy on me. I'm an unlucky star, I bring misery. I have at least one consolation: never having lied to you. In a few years, I'll be all alone, abandoned. I'll remember then what I lost in you. I'll pay in bitter tears, but it will be too late. You'll have your revenge. Adieu! A little courage will save you from a life of regret. Forgive me!

Céleste

I called for my maid and gave her this letter. Robert slept on. Sweat dripped from his forehead; he was unsettled. I didn't want a single tear to be over me. I was only too aware that I didn't deserve it.

Robert's illness didn't change his personality. He worked himself into a rage against me for no reason. Sometimes he rang for his valet so he wouldn't have to ask me for his tincture, which was next to me. He told me to leave, that my presence horrified him. I would cry without answering, so he would ask my forgiveness for his outbursts, kiss my hands, and say, "I love you more than my own life. If

I could no longer see you, I would go insane!"

His robust nature triumphed over illness. After several days, he was on the mend. He let me go home after making me promise to come back soon.

I found four letters from Richard at my apartment. The first read:

Why did I meet you, Céleste? I don't mean to insult you or blame you. I reserve that for the man who you prefer to me. What he loves in you, that's me. When I am at the end of a world of a torment that I can no longer bear, that's when he'll break up with you, sure that I won't be glad to take you back anymore. Mark my words, and maybe you'll think of me when it happens. Remember that I offered you my life, my name, and that no other love could compare to mine. It's not enough to abandon me to my despair, you have to insult me by offering to send back the money that I was so happy to give you. If you pay it back to me, I'll give it to the poor. You could almost buy back that fateful day from your past with that much money. Keep it. It's all that I ask of you in parting.

I'm going to stay with one of my sisters. I don't have the strength to go through this. I spent four days beneath the windows at rue Royale, always hoping to see you behind a curtain. Those days were long. I'd rather die than start all over again.

The other letters were like this one, always sweet and full of regrets.

My mother came to see me. When she had nothing else to do, she remembered I existed. She told me all of her problems. After having promised me that she wouldn't see Vincent anymore, I promised that I would buy her a tobacco shop or a building with furnished rooms to let, in hopes that this would keep her busy. This sounded good to her, and three days later I set her up with a place on rue Cléry.

Three months went by.

Robert was horribly depressed. He was physically fine, but he had a pain deep inside his heart that was eating him alive. My trip to London came into his mind constantly. A dress, a word, reminded him. Then he fell into such a depressed state of mind that his smile caused me pain. Richard was with his family this whole time. I shook at the thought of his return to Paris, because that would be still worse. My only fights with Robert were over the gifts he wouldn't stop giving me. He tried in vain to curb his spending, and he found it annoying. The merchants who sold to him, these expert swindlers, rolled over his loans at each due date and in two years had doubled his balance for him.

One day, one of his relatives came to see me. He was a large man, and very religious. Though he made clear his interest in Robert, he hadn't given him so much as twenty-five louis. But he was generous with advice.

"Look," he said to me, "you love Robert? Fine. But you don't prove it to him at all. How can you let him ruin himself like a naïve idiot? Tell him to get married. What are you going to do when he no longer has an inheritance? Reason with him a little. He'll listen to you. If misfortune comes to him, I'll be sorry, but I won't give him a sou. I have bills to pay."

"My God!" I said to him. "He's not asking for anything from you. I'll tell him of your concern for him and try to make him understand your side."

That evening, I spoke to Robert about his future.

"I'm afraid for you. I'm more practical now. If you want to get married, I won't stand in your way. I'll leave Paris if my being here bothers you. You can write me kind letters, and I'll answer with my whole heart. We'll move from this great love to a friendship that will last forever."

"Oui," he said, "you're right. Tell me what to do. But I want to see you, to have you nearby in the future. We'll go to Berry together. We'll buy a little house where you can put all your things and that allows you to come visit me in the country."

That made sense, and we left town a few days later. We found a delicious little cottage whose lawn backed up onto the forest. It was impossible to hunt without my hearing the sound of the horn and the howling of the dogs.

My presence in the country had a bad effect on Robert's new plans. He tasked himself with arranging my hermitage, and I went back to Paris.

When I got home, I had to see my mother. She hadn't found anything better to do than rent the first-floor apartment of her building to M. Vincent. Rage overtook me, and I gave them both a piece of my mind. I took back the building immediately.

I wrote to Robert, who was horribly bored in Berry, but he remained there to prove to everyone that he wasn't seeing me anymore.

I started to take pleasure in being alone. I was calm. But it wasn't my destiny to settle my emotions. When one bout of boredom passed, another came on.

One day, at four o'clock, my maid announced M. Richard. I stayed in my armchair. I didn't want to welcome him in nor to give him an excuse, like that I was under the weather. He gave me his hand without reproach.

"My dear Céleste, I've come. Believe me when I say that I have heard. I have been assured that M. Robert is at his grounds in the country, and I am presenting myself at your apartment in hopes that you will always have a little friendship for me. But since the heart of a woman is a pit that can never be sounded, I believe I was too hopeful. I will go."

I was released from my fear. I had been expecting an argument, but what he said was not embarrassing at all.

"You are and will always be welcome. I was afraid that you'd shame me, and since I knew I deserved it, I didn't want to hear it."

"I would never do that to you. There's no fight possible between us. Non, Céleste, I will not get tired of your complaints, no matter how irritating. I'll wait. I'll still love you ten years from today."

I was showered with love, adored. But I couldn't keep myself from laughing. I didn't think that love could last ten years.

"I don't ask anything of you but to come see you sometimes."

"Certainly, as often as you like."

This last bit was unwise of me to say, and here's the proof. I still wrote to Robert, but I didn't think it necessary to inform him of Richard's return to Paris. I don't know who did think it was necessary or how he found out.

⁂

One day, I asked Maria to dinner. This is a new character who deserves her own description, so I'll tell you how I came to know her.

Maria was a tall woman with strong, pretty features, but she was stringy and extremely thin. I had known her since the days when I was going to Versailles. I reconnected with her at a ball at the Odéon given by M. Lireux, the theater director at the time. He was very good to the women; he brought them together as a group, walked into the dance rehearsal, chose his dancers, and brought them to supper in the artists' green room. I should tell you, to protect his reputation, that there were never fewer than forty people at these events.

I went to this masked ball with Marie le Blonde. Her lover planned to meet her there; as always, he stood her up. Monrose, who I knew slightly, had requested that I dine with the other artists. M. Lireux welcomed me warmly. I had on a pretty dress, and I remember that I was the guest of honor that evening. On my right was a fat woman with gaping nostrils and bulging eyes. This was Clara Fontaine. She was looking jealously at Maria's outfit. She traveled in the same circles. They were like two prostitutes in the Latin Quarter who should have everything in common, but when one is dressed better than the other, the latter takes her revenge by being nasty.

The supper was magnificent. They served as much pâté de foie gras, truffles, and champagne as you could want. Maria had a serious attitude in the midst of these fiery personalities. She ate carefully, because she kept her gloves on.

Clara, who thought "anything goes" because it was Carnival season, said to her in a pointedly polite voice, "Why do you eat with your gloves on? Do you have mange?"

Poor Maria turned white, then purple, unable to say a word. Tears came to her eyes.

I found this so rude that, though I only knew Maria by sight, I took up her defense. I said to Clara, "Why do you ask if she has mange? Do you think you gave it to her?"

"Moi!" she said in shock. She placed her two huge hands on the table to show there was no trace.

"Put those away," I said. "They're not appropriate in polite company."

She closed her mouth and flared her nostrils without finding a word to say to me.

Maria came over to thank me.

Lireux, Monrose, and Bernard-Latte—who were still boys then; they've married since, I believe—said I was right. And Maria became my friend.

Across from me sat M. Milon, the actor. He seemed like a blowhard to me. His demeanor was too studied. He looked at himself in any reflection and seemed so pleased with himself that I left my seat to get out of the way of the mirror that was behind me.

I asked Maria if she danced. She was wearing a man's suit, and she wore it with insouciance. I don't even know what kind of dance I was doing. I stepped on the foot of a woman in a domino mask who was behind me. She shoved me—hard—and called me an ox. She'd said it without thinking; at least she hadn't called me a monster, though she hated me. So she tried again and called me a horror of a woman.

I turned around and pulled on her mask's beard, saying, "You're pretty, actually, for a monkey." Then I laughed and said, "Look at how madame has to turn up her nose to call me a horror!"

My God, what had I done. There was only one woman in the whole hall who mattered, the one who had called me a beast. And I had unmasked her.

In a fury, she looked around for the host.

I was asked to leave. I didn't, and that was not the right thing to do, because I was asked to go by the police station.

That's what made me want to run. I prepared myself to say to this woman that I found her absolutely tremendous. Luckily for me, Louis Monrose, who was as good a guy as he was an actor, came to my rescue. I was starting to be very afraid. He proved to the host that if this woman hadn't put her foot beneath mine, I wouldn't have stepped on it. He got me a pardon and brought me upstairs.

Lireux laughed at my story and remained my friend for a long time. We often went to see him because he had huge crates of oranges in his pantry. They were so good. I was allowed to carry off six of them at a time.

That's how I came to know Maria. Then I lost track of her until she started to be known as Maria la Polkeuse and I was Céleste Mogador. She was the daughter of a laborer. They say that everyone has their faults, and I had too many. If Maria had one, it was her height.

If I'm allowed to speak of my good friends this way, it's because they're not bothered by my saying these things—not even my ex-friends who treated me very badly when I later debuted at Variétés in the *Course au Plaisir*. The oranges were swapped out for stones.

But at that time, Maria rivaled the peacock for pride. She was very elegant and walked along the Champs-Élysées in velvet dresses. And when I ran into her by chance while leaving the Hippodrome, she looked at me from the height of her grandeur without even saying hello. This didn't hurt me, since I'd created a little philosophy for myself regarding the opinions of other women.

She found that her name didn't fit so well under a feathered hat, so she changed it to Saint-Pose. She was that embarrassed that she had to choose a new name.

"Oh," I said to her, "you're not called Maria anymore?"

"Never call me anything," she said to me.

I told her frankly that she should get used to it, because as it was, everyone was saying it anyway: "There goes Maria la Polkeuse."

She became apoplectic. When she had regained her composure, she said, "Whatever. I know who I am."

A month later I asked her concierge if she was home, and he said he didn't know her. I sank into a bad mood as I left the building. Luckily, she was sitting at the window and remembered me.

"Why are you leaving?"

"He told me that he didn't know who you were!"

"Oh, right. That's because I'm called Mme. la comtesse Marie de Bussy now."

When I went upstairs, I saw that she had taken her name seriously. Everything in the room had a crown on it.

"Well, Maria, would you like my opinion on your name change and your coat of arms?"

"Oui."

"You give the impression of being fickle and dressed by a costume designer. Though these things are all lovely when you get them, they make you seem ridiculous when you flaunt them without having any right to them. You're a good girl, and I love you very much. That's why I'm giving you advice. When people see a woman like us, they know what she is. You can't lie to others as easily as you lie to yourself."

My opinion was apparently stupid because she arrived at my house for lunch in a carriage emblazoned with *three crowns* the size of the moon.

At five o'clock one day, with her place at the table set, Richard came to pay me a visit. A knock sounded behind him, and I assumed it was her, so I asked Richard to let her in. It was Robert.

I lost control of my senses and I couldn't find a single word to say.

"Well!" said Robert when he saw the two place settings on the table. "I now know what I came to find out." Then turning to Richard, he said, "You wanted to marry this woman. Don't make such a foolish move. You'll pay for it, and it's not worth the sacrifice. I'll leave her to you. She's yours from here on."

Robert's lesson did not make Richard happy. His face twitched. Robert stood there, pinning him with a staring eye. I thought I was going to die. Something awful was about to happen if I didn't find a way to sidestep it.

I clasped my hands and looked at Richard. He understood, because he said to Robert coldly, "Thank you for your opinion, monsieur. You've known her, I believe, for four years? Well, in four years, I will have an answer for you."

Robert left, throwing me a hateful glance as he did, and I returned it from the bottom of my heart.

I asked Richard to let me be alone.

Maria arrived. She did all she could to console me. Bad luck was headed my way, and I ran right in front of it. If Maria was a bit silly, she also had redeeming qualities. She came to see me over the next several days and tried to shoo away my depression with kind words.

Robert, to save face after this meeting at my place,

went in search of a woman he could be seen with in polite society. He found a country girl in a hotel dining room who had been brought to Paris by a gentleman in exchange for an undisclosed sum. She knew that Robert had a mistress he loved and that she was only serving to make another woman jealous. She accepted this role and filled it with relish. To tell the truth, I have to admit she was pretty.

Richard visited repeatedly to tell me, "I ran into your Robert with his mistress. He'd have to do better than that to replace you." He had no idea how much this hurt me.

Maria, for her part, came to tell me, "Oh, that. Your Robert is insane. He's going around town with a woman in an open carriage, and what a woman! She's as interesting as a bale of hay."

It all hit at the same place and the same time. The depression could not have been worse. The bile that was turned toward me overflowed in someone else's direction.

Naturally, that someone was Richard, who I'd decided to hate. I blamed him for everything that had gone wrong. He asked for my forgiveness for things he hadn't done.

Then I received a note from Robert. He had bought a magnificent apartment from someone who was leaving town. Everything was ready, and he had moved in. He wrote: "Come see me. I have to speak to you about something that is in your interest."

Richard arrived while I was reading this note, and without knowing what it contained, he said, "Your Robert spouts all kinds of colorful nonsense about you. He told one of my friends yesterday that you'll be at his place anytime he wants."

I angrily tore up the letter.

When Richard had gone, I wrote back.

What would I do at your house? Come looking to be insulted? You never loved me. You don't say such things about people you love, and I know everything you think and say about me. Adieu!
  Céleste

An hour later, he wrote me again:

You're lying when you say I never loved you. You know perfectly well that it's just the opposite. You've said slanderous things about me. I tried to save myself from the ridicule that you cynically threw at me. I wanted to see you for one second at my place, to lift myself out of the despair caused by your declared hate for me. I carry the end of all suffering in my fingertip: I want to end up between the bottle that doesn't lie and that provides the drink it promises, and the pistol that will allow me to forget. One day, when I pay you back, I'll send all my letters to you. They were the essence of my heart and my life. I read yours with happiness. I forgot what you are. I dreamed of you and adored you. Enjoy the good life, but beware: You'll grow old fast. And when the heart, which does not age, needs care and affection, it is awful to have only memories of hatred and disdain.
  Robert

It was like an express train that day. I was not alone for a minute. In their attempts to distract me, everyone overwhelmed me.

I told myself, as I hid away the letter, *I'll be at Robert's tomorrow.*

39

"Come to Cirque," Richard said to me. "It will take your mind off things. There's a good show on."

I dressed after dinner, and we left at eight o'clock.

The room was splendid, filled with lights and fashion. I was depressed. It all seemed somber to me. All of a sudden, the room lit up. My eyes were blinded. The noise of my blood boiling in my heart drowned out the sound of the orchestra. My pupils, as if dilated by belladonna, stared without seeing. My head spun, and I felt myself sway in my seat like a ship on the sea.

Richard looked at me, then took me by the arm, gripping me as if he were angry. "Why are you so pale? Sit down, or you'll be sick."

I made an effort. I lifted my head, which had been battered by a vision, and found myself face to face with Robert. He too was ashen. He was seated to the side of me, but higher up. He began to chat with this woman I'd heard so much about, undoubtedly about me. She began to speak loudly and animatedly to get my attention. As she spoke, she came so near his face that I thought she was about to kiss him! I couldn't handle it anymore. I asked Richard to take me home.

"Non," he said. "If I have any right to ask you for something in exchange for what I've done for you, then please at least pretend to have a good time for the rest of the show."

I didn't say a word. I watched with a terrified stare as the horses went around in front of me.

Richard said, "Look, Céleste, I beg of you, spare a thought for me. You know that I've always done well for myself. But today, in front of everyone, don't make a fool of me. Rein it in, just for an hour. I can see that you're miserable. I get it. But I'm just as miserable as you are. You look exhausted. Your eyes are full of tears about to fall. Céleste, Céleste, I'm begging you!"

I heard everything he said. He was right. But I could not get out from under this depression, which was stronger than I ever imagined it could be. He squeezed my hand harder. I came back to myself a little and began to laugh like a madwoman who's off her rocker.

"Let's go," Richard said. "You've done enough for me today. We're leaving. Come on, I'm going to take you home."

I got up, and my knees buckled. I leaned on his arm. I looked at Robert, and his eyes again met Richard's. I felt a shiver, as if the blades of two cold swords had crossed over my heart.

I let myself be taken home like a child. I was paralyzed without knowing where this illness that was making me so insane came from.

When we got to my door, Richard said, "Adieu, Céleste. Thank you again. I'll leave you; your sadness needs to be alone. My friends are waiting for me at la Maison-d'Or. I'd offer to bring you along, but you need to rest." And with that, he left me.

Once I was alone, my fever returned with full force. I picked up the last letter from Robert: He would always love me, according to what he wrote. "I'll end up between a bottle of wine, which holds what it promises—drunkenness—and a pistol, which lets me forget." But this woman, why does he have her? To save himself from what he calls ridicule. He doesn't love her. He refuses to marry her because he doesn't have the courage to say to anyone else, I love you! Tomorrow I'll go see him.

I went to bed, hoping to find a little calm in sleep. But it was in vain. My heart bled out from all sides. The blood rushed to my brain, and the delirium made me stronger. I got up and got dressed, as if a voice were calling me from outside.

"Louise," I said to my maid, "come with me. Don't leave me alone, no matter what happens. My sanity is going; let's run after it, or I'll be lost." I picked up the letter that had Robert's new address and made my way along the boulevards.

When I got to rue Joubert, I stopped, afraid of what I was about to do. I wanted to retrace my steps, but my good sense did not obey me, and I knocked on the outer door. It was almost one in the morning. The door opened, and I went up without asking for Robert, leaving Louise at the door.

At the first floor, I knocked hard enough to make the whole house shake. No one answered. This was both joy and pain. There was no one home, or they didn't want to answer. So much the better. What would I have said? I went to go back down; that was the reasonable thing to do. But madness has no reason, and since I knew where the bell cord was, I paid ten times over to ring it.

I heard a door open, then footsteps, and a voice—Robert's—asking, "Who's there?"

My tongue froze. I leaned against the wall so I wouldn't fall.

"Who's there?" he said again as he opened the front door. Illuminating my face with his candle, he said, "You! Here! At this hour! What do you want?"

I had no idea how to answer. I saw such sarcasm on his face that I knew he was going to take his revenge on me.

"Look," he said, "I don't have time to waste. What do you have to say to me?"

"Me," I said, shaking as I held out the letter. "I came because you wrote to me yesterday!"

"Oh!" he laughed. "That's right, I did, after lunch. If that's all, you can go home. There's no danger. I'm fine. How come M. Richard let you out at this hour? It's not wise. I'd forbid it."

The mocking way he said all this lowered me, little by little, toward my violent tendencies. The depression in my heart moved over to be replaced by a massive rage. He saw the flashes in my eyes and was, if possible, even more enraging.

"Come in," he said as he moved out of the doorframe. "I don't love you anymore. You bring far too much chaos. But I'm too polite not to invite you in to rest for a minute." He put his candle on the table and offered me a seat.

The room we entered was a dining room with paneling and sculpted moldings. It showcased the luxury and taste of other people. I looked around while I fixed my expression because I didn't dare say a word.

"It seems," he said, "that this is a visit without a goal, my dear Céleste. You've chosen a bad time, my child, because I'm not alone. But, since you've come, I'll tell you where I stand and the state of my heart so that in the future we can avoid such meetings. I was amorous with you, or at least I think so. You made a fool of yourself over me. I'm tired of this embarrassing role and just don't love you anymore. The sight of you disgusts me because it reminds me of my everlasting shame. Go find M. Richard."

As he spoke, his eyes became frightening. I clasped my hands and said, "Look, Robert, don't talk down to me. Drop the mockery that turns me to ice, listen to me for five minutes, and then I'll go. I was wrong to come; you must forgive me. It's a stronger power than my will that's driving me. How could I tell that this letter only contained lies and illusions? You wrote of killing yourself; I came. You saw me again; I came."

"Non," he said. "You didn't come for my sake. You came because you saw me with another woman, because you wanted to risk your entire empire for me. Fine! Here's my answer: She's over there, this woman, just behind that door. She's listening to everything I'm telling you. I love her. She is beautiful, as beautiful as you are ugly. People say she looks like you, and that's why I chose her. Maybe! But you're a mere imitation of her."

"Robert," and I left my body as I spoke, "Robert, what you've done is cowardly. You insult me at your house. You should have more respect for yourself and not insult weaker opponents. If you need to make love to this woman so you can tell me about it, she better take note, because the same thing is waiting for her down the road. If I've fucked up one of your nights of pleasure, I have that right, because you fucked up my life. Why did you write to me in London? Without that letter, I'd be married today. I'd be in Scotland. I wouldn't bother you anymore. I know perfectly what you love in me: yourself! I can't believe it, because I have a more generous soul than you know. I broke up with you so you could marry and so I wouldn't be an accomplice to your almost certain ruin. I accepted another man's proposal that I didn't want, nor did I ask for or accept a proposal from you. The idea only occurred to me when you took another mistress. You promised me that as soon as you married, when you were entirely over me, that's when I would want to help you. You cannot blame me; I've been avoiding you. You lied to me when you wrote this letter. Ah! I'm losing my mind... Be careful, don't say word, because I'm about to commit a crime! The flame from this light is red, and everything is turning that color. Adieu... never see me again, disappear...I will do everything I can to get you out of my life... It would take more than your money, your life, your honor, to make me forget this night! I would give my life if you would love me again in six months."

I went to leave, and he blocked my way.

"Non," he said, "you're too worked up. You can't leave yet. Anger looks good on you; I want to see where this goes! You tell me to never come back to you... Calm down, I've made my decision, and I'll stick to it. I look down on you, a miserable creature that I picked out of the gutter and who has dirtied my name in return. I was only a ladder for you. It was funny to see a man of good standing in love with a girl like you, to see him bring her to his house, to see his curiosity piqued. You were put on a pedestal, and you sold yourself to the highest bidder."

I looked around for some way to defuse this fight. I saw a knife on the sideboard. I grabbed it and, gripping it tight, yelled, "Not another word, Robert. Let me be, or I'll kill you."

He crossed his arms and leaned his back against the door. "Finally," he said, laughing. "I want to see you suffer a little. I thought you were made of stone. Put down the knife, you're going to cut your fingers."

"You think I won't drive this blade into your heart, like you drove your cruel words into mine? You think I'm too weak? You think I'm afraid of death? Fine! Do what I say, or I'll kill you. Go get this woman who's heard everything you said to me!"

He shrugged but didn't move.

"You don't believe me! Wait, I'll start with myself so you have no doubt." And I stabbed myself twice in the chest. The cold blade slid down my side, leaving a scratch. Rending my flesh was less awful than the rending of my heart.

Robert didn't see the blood and assumed I was faking. He came toward me to take the knife.

"Get away," I said. "Let me go." When he didn't back off fast enough, I stabbed his right arm. His blood flowed. As soon as I saw it, I realized I had gone completely off the rails and apologized.

"I forgive you," he said, "but don't leave."

I took a few steps and put my hand to my chest. I felt a slow boil, then the cold of my breast. I put one hand on the table to steady myself and with the other tried to stop the blood. I lost my life and my strength. My head spun, my heart stopped beating, and I fell to the floor.

When I came to, I was in a large room decorated in red velvet with gold trim. I was stretched out on a bed from François I covered in double white satin and surrounded by four golden columns. There were two candles lit in a large golden candelabra that could hold at least twenty. My chest was cold. I placed my hand to staunch the bleeding. A large sponge had been placed there. I'd been given vinegar to drink, which had caused a violent illness. My maid had been brought up, and she was seated in an upholstered chair. I listened, holding my breath, because someone was speaking in the next room.

"I beg your pardon, my dear friend," Robert was saying, "to have made you spend such a horrible night... You must be cold... As soon as dawn comes, I'll go look for a carriage and put her in it. Her wound is not serious... Rest will do her good."

I remembered everything, and I wept.

Robert came to my bedside and said, "Feeling better? Yes, you're insane, dear child, to pick a fight like that with me. It seems to me that I never disturbed you like this. If I wrote you, you should have burned my letters without reading them. You are not a child; you knew what you were doing when you broke up with me. I want to be free."

I looked at the open door. This woman heard everything. "Oui," I said, "you're right. Close the door. I'm going. Louise, come help me get dressed."

He left the room. I heard him laughing—at me, no doubt. My heart broke all over again. I no longer had the strength to do anything but cry. I wanted to get up, but I couldn't. I had to stay in bed and inhale vinegar.

Louise called out, "Madame is not well!"

The woman I had seen at Cirque came in and spoke to Robert; she had a noticeable accent. I thought she came in more out of curiosity than sincere concern. She had short, curly hair. She looked a lot like one of the first friends I ever had.

There are certain people who make you feel even more humiliated. I didn't have anything to say to her. I didn't know her. I only asked her to leave the room while I got ready to go. She did, laughing, and I heard her kiss Robert.

I don't know where I found the strength—in my hatred, no doubt—but I left this room that looked like a tomb. He didn't even shake my hand as I went.

It was daylight. Louise carried me more than I walked. I stopped on the other side of the street. The window was open, surely to assure him that I was far away. After he'd seen me go, Robert closed it again.

We didn't come across a carriage. I headed for home, my body broken but my mind alert. This memory, which passed through my heart like a red-hot iron, burned me. It only cooled a little with thoughts of revenge. Poor Richard! So good, so devoted, and I had mistreated him. This was my punishment. But it would hurt him so badly if I told him about this fight, a fight that I couldn't deny because I had an enormous bandage across my chest.

"You need to go to bed, madame" Louise said. "I'm going to look for a doctor."

"Non," I said. "I have an obligation to fulfill. I have to tell Richard. It's better that he hears this news from me. Oh! I lack the strength! Go to his place, and tell him to come quickly."

She left. *I've lost too much blood…I'm deathly pale. My God! Take my life. It's too much.*

40

Louise returned to the house.

"Oh madame," she said, "the concierge at Richard's is crazy. He didn't want to let me go upstairs, he said, 'There's no one there. M. Richard has gone out with madame.' 'But,' I said to him, 'Madame is at her house. She's the one who sent me!' He stood firm and said, 'Mademoiselle, I beg of you. Oh, hell. I'm so stupid. It's not her upstairs; the other woman is the same height as her. Don't say anything to madame.' I promised not to say anything, but I thought you should be informed of this, because without Richard, the fight tonight wouldn't have happened."

"Ah!" I cried in a state of delirium just this side of madness. "It's awful to live like this. Why wasn't I strangled as soon as I came into the world? Why are there woeful creatures like me on this earth? We're the shame of our parents and cause anyone who loves us shame and degradation. Does anyone love a girl like me? Sometimes you forget when you're around them; then after she's damned, she's chased away and told the truth. Well done, Robert. I am so unworthy! My God, why won't you let me die?" I removed the compresses on my wounds with such force that my nails scratched my skin. I would have done more, but just as it had on rue Geoffrey-Marie, my strength left me. I fell into a chair and wanted to cry, but my eyelashes were dry and burning.

Nothing! I said to myself. *He's nothing to me. I hope he never comes back to me, that his love dies, because I will take my revenge!*

Robert! He had no concern for me. The way he treated me in front of that woman! Like he was grinding me to dust under his heel. As if he could look down on me! And Richard, who retracted his friendship when I needed it most. I lost everything all at once.

I was alone in the world.

Louise came into my room and said, "Madame, the wet nurse is here with your goddaughter. I told her that you were resting and I didn't know if you'd be able to see her."

"Oui," I said, "have them come in." She reminded me that even if I had no one who loved me, I was the only person in the entire world that this poor baby had.

My little girl was brought to me. She was delicate as a flower. I looked for life in her eyes, but I only saw weakness and exhaustion. My heart found more tears. However, the woman who was keeping her assured me that she was doing well. I had to force myself to smile to get her to perk up. The poor angel rewarded me for the effort, because she matched me kiss for kiss. When they had gone, I felt restored. Her presence had done me good, even in my soul. I wanted to forget everything else, to think only of her, but I couldn't. Her memory dimmed my depression but didn't cure it.

Louise came back in to ask me if I wanted to see M. Richard.

"Did he say anything to you? Does he know that you went to his house this morning?"

"I don't think so, madame. He didn't say anything about it to me."

"Good. Let him in."

I sat in a shadow so that he couldn't see my face. He came in and crossed over to me to take my hand. I motioned for him to sit opposite me.

"Well, my dear Richard, how was the rest of your evening, your dinner at Maison d'Or? Did it go on very late?"

"Non," he said, "I was home by midnight. You know I get bored when you're not there."

"Ah. And you came here straight from your place?"

"Oui," he said calmly, which weakened my resolve to not tell him what I knew.

"Wait, I was told that you met someone this morning, outside?"

He changed color and said, "Actually, I went out very early to try out a horse, but I went right home after."

"Dear Richard, what a sad night you've had. You love me to the point of being jealous of my thoughts?"

"Oui, I had a bad night. I kept thinking that no matter how much I love you, I'm unable to make you happy."

"Come on," I said, "enough pretending and making faces. Tell me the name of the woman who consoled you during this long, sad night."

The blood drained from his face.

"Don't search your brain for a story, it's no use. I know everything except the name of the woman. I want to know! No wasted words, a single word: her name. And I'll forgive you."

"Oh, Céleste," he said, falling to his knees in front of me. "You don't mean it, you don't forgive me. Oui, I am a madman, I lost my senses, but I love you more than my life. I proved it to you, Céleste. Forgive a drunken moment. Yesterday, at dinner, I was out of my mind, and you'd hurt me so badly. This woman, she seduced me. Céleste, forgive me. Drop this icy air that makes me ill. Yell at me, I deserve it. But forgive me."

"I asked you for her name. I want to know if it's one of my close friends so I can compliment her for her good taste."

"Non, you won't know her. I'll never see her again. I should never have seen her in the first place. She doesn't know all the trouble that she's caused me today."

"You're crying! A man! That's pushing the lie too far. You saw Robert with a woman, and you said to yourself, *He broke up with her, I can break up with her too*. You're only fooling yourself when you say you love me; you love her. I don't want your love, I don't love you, I never loved you, and you know it. Look, don't cry like that, you're getting on my nerves. I'm not going to yell at you; you're free to do what you want. I know well enough to wish you happiness with another. Is she pretty?"

"Céleste, Céleste, you are merciless. You have no heart."

"Mercy. Did anyone have mercy for me last night? Don't I have a heart? I did, until it hurt me." And I told him the story of all that had happened, and why I sent my maid to look for him. He was so good that he didn't even blame me, he only tried to apologize.

"You asked for the name of the woman. It's Adèle Célier."

"I've seen her a couple of times. She's pretty. Tall and blonde, right? You have good taste."

"Céleste, you are cruel."

"Why? Because you didn't make a scene? I'll only miss one thing from you: your friendship. I'm the one who should be asking your forgiveness. I'll never forget what you did for me. Stay with her, and don't come here anymore. If you still love me, I'll only hurt you without meaning to. The world is inhumane. We're happy to inflict the harm on others that's been done to us. Don't be the victim."

"Non, non, I don't want to leave you." He clutched my hands and covered them in tears. "I'll kill myself if you don't forgive me."

"Come on, I already asked you not to say such stupid things. You don't want to break up with me, you'll take me in your arms, you'll go everywhere with me. But I have the right to leave you behind no matter where we go. You'll no longer be my friend. Don't ask me for a kind word; I'm incapable of saying one. Leave. When you get downstairs, ask for my carriage to be brought around. I have to go out, I need some air. I feel like I'm going to die. Come back for me at nine o'clock. I want to go to Ranelagh."

When I was alone, I dressed in all my best things. I used blush to hide how pale I was. I got into the carriage so well turned out that everyone stopped and said as I went by, "How happy that woman is!" When I came to the Champs-Élysées, many people seemed surprised to see me. Finally some stopped me to say, "Wait, you're not dead? I heard you'd killed yourself last night. You really seemed like you might do it." I endured twenty conversations like this.

All my acquaintances knew what had happened, and everyone wanted to see the other woman who had led Mogador to stab herself with a knife. Robert threatened to get revenge on M. Richard and said to whoever would listen, "It's unbearable, these women are picking me apart."

I made a point of going wherever I could tell my story. I made sure to look as rich as possible, which Richard encouraged by supplying me with the loveliest things.

Robert came to see me one morning. He tried to seem aloof as he said, "I came to find out how you're doing."

"In short, it was useless for you to come. You annoy me. I'm waiting for M. Richard, and you know I'm doing well. You need no longer fear for me, so what did you come to see?"

"You're looking well. Would you serve me lunch? There's a place set."

"I'm sorry to say no, but I'm expecting someone."

"Oh, so you're seeing him again."

"And what would you do in exchange?"

"I'll send my lodger away."

At this, I felt my heart leap, but I couldn't tell if it

was with hate or joy. "For sure?" I asked.

"For sure."

"So be it. It's a deal."

Richard knocked, and I opened the door. I asked him not to come in.

"Go," I said. "Go back to Mlle. Adele. I told you that I'd use my freedom when I needed to. Robert is here. Today, I can tell you the truth: I'm not following my heart, but my sense of worth."

"Adieu," he said. "You'll never see me again."

I paid no attention to this word that's repeated so often. Besides, I was too preoccupied with my revenge.

Robert tried to explain himself. He spoke as if his every word was a victory, yet I remained sweet and humble. He believed I'd been broken for good, because I said a prayer that he would stay with me.

"I love you the tiniest bit," he said, "but I'm the only one. I don't know what you've done to all these other women; everyone detests you. Judith wrote me—she cannot bear you. All these snide remarks are exhausting, and I have to pick a side. I see you from time to time, but we each maintain our independence."

"I don't know, my dear friend, why Mlle. Judith would write to you about me. I only know her by sight."

"She swears that you wrote to her for an invitation to her place, and that she refused you."

"Truly, my dear Robert, I'm astonished that you, an intelligent man, would pay attention to the clucking of this woman. I've already told you that I only sent such a note to one woman, to make her lie, and that's Ozy. Since you're corresponding with Mlle. Judith, why hasn't she shown you my letter?"

"I don't see her; I don't think I've even spoken to

her. I don't know how we started writing to each other. What I remember is that she told me in a letter that I shouldn't be so proud of my conquest, that the taking of Mogador didn't start only yesterday. I responded that after having consulted ancient and modern historians, I had discovered that Judith had put Holofernes's head in a bag a long time ago, but not so long before the taking of Mogador. She sent the letter back. I didn't know what this meant, and I didn't bother to find out. To show you that I'm not lying, I'll bring you these letters."

He did in fact give them to me much later. I have them, and I didn't understand the reason for this slander either.

Lunch was served.

Robert had a lightness that made me sick.

"Come on," he said, "stop looking like you're at a funeral. I'm going to give some money to this woman who's staying at my place, have her rent an apartment, and I'll come get you for dinner at six o'clock. You'll see that I'm not worried about you!"

"Fine," I said, "but don't forget that I have the right to come find you, and I will."

He went out. A few minutes later, I was brought a letter from Richard.

I told you, Céleste, that I would not see you anymore. You understand that to keep this promise, I have to leave town—far away, very far. One of my friends is going to California, and I'm going with him. I know you better than you know yourself. You have hate and bile in your heart. The terrible way you've been treated by others has made you this way. You are a good person. In the state you're in, you need to heal yourself by doing to someone all

that they've done to you. I'm giving you the chance to not waste it on me anymore. You've put yourself in a prison made of cruelty. If it were only that, I wouldn't leave. I'd hide myself as you passed, and I could watch you from afar. But I wasn't honest with you about my status. I'm broke. It's up to me to pay my own way. Losing you is the only thing that makes me sad. I'll be back in a few years, and I'll still be the same. If I'm rich, I'll ask you if you need me. Adieu, I love you. I only ever loved you, and will only ever love you…
Richard

This news terrified me. His leaving meant nothing to me, but his ruin horrified me. Poor boy! What would become of him? I immediately wrote to him to offer whatever I had. A response came via my maid that he had left his rooms that same day, and he hadn't left a letter for me with the concierge. Remorse hurt me to my core. Robert was the cause of this misery as much as me. Maybe he was my unwilling accomplice, but that's the result of his whims. He would have to take care of himself and not laugh off everything that happened. I would use him to get back at Richard.

I waited until six o'clock with my mind on fire. The bell rang, and Robert didn't arrive.

I paced the room impatiently, nervously. I said to myself, He's not going to come. He toyed with my despair. He has what he wanted. Richard gave up his place to him, and he's laughing at what he's done. And I let him savor this triumph with that woman in the next room! He didn't believe it, he can't believe it!

Seven o'clock!

"Louise, bring me a cape and hat."

"Madame," the girl said, "please, don't go out when you're like this."

"Have no fear, I'm in no danger." And I left.

When I came to rue Joubert, I found the valet. He'd known me a long time. I was the one who had asked him to come in at Robert's country house.

"Where is your master?" I asked him.

"He's gone out, madame. He went to dinner, but he'll be back early. He's throwing a party. He told me he would return at eight o'clock."

"Good. And that woman is with him?"

"Oui, madame."

"Where are her things?"

"There, in the small bedroom."

"Light the lamps for me."

I went into the room, where I found a large trunk and dresses strewn about. I went to put everything into the trunk, and I ordered the valet to take it to the hotel de Princes. He did.

"Now," I said, "my dear Robert, for the three of us. First, us two."

I opened his pistol case with the firm resolve to fire a bullet into his brain and kill myself after if he didn't do as I said. Luckily for him, I couldn't find any bullets. When his carriage pulled up, I went to the window. I saw him near an open phaeton, taking that woman into his arms to help her step out. My blood boiled, and I would have killed him—oh, I am sure of it. He'd never get into that carriage again. I had a talent rare for a woman: I could hit nineteen flies with twenty bullets. I was known for my strength, which did not falter that day. My mind was cold, but it did not shiver.

I waited for them in the salon. Everything was lit up

for the party. The walls were covered in white-and-gold-stamped leather; the furniture was upholstered in green brocade. The mirrors reflected the candles, and the thick white wool carpets with red and green flowers muffled the sound of my footsteps. I could only hear my heart. When a latch was pushed, a door covered in mirrors opened to the side of a mural. This apartment had been decorated for Mlle. Rachel. Everything brought the taste of the great artist to mind.

Robert appeared and stopped, considering. No one had dared tell him I was there.

"Are you surprised to see me? Did you forget about me?"

He was still confused.

His companion came in. She looked at me and listened without comprehending as I addressed her.

"He didn't tell you that he came to my place this morning, that he had come to ask me to dinner? He should have warned you. It would have been polite. Tell madame, then, that I am not lying. You can see she's skeptical."

"It's true," said Robert. He didn't dare defy me beneath the weight of my stare. "I was going to bring her your news. I promised you what you asked of me, Céleste, but I thought about it, and then I wasn't able to see madame between this morning and this evening. It took me time to find her someplace convenient to stay."

"Fine!" I said. "But it seems to me that you found her at the hotel des Princes, and that didn't take much time at all. I thought you were serious, so I came to secure this apartment and had all her trunks sent along."

Robert was entirely dumbstruck.

The poor country mouse just looked stupid.

At last Robert found his words. "Look, Céleste, I beg you, no scenes, no violence. I promise that madame will leave tomorrow. She knows she cannot stay with me, but I'm entertaining guests tonight."

"And you ask me to leave! You truly make me laugh. I warned you, I told you: Don't come back to me. You came back. You made a date. It's not a promise you have any right to break. That was the deal. I paid, and Richard has taken off. As for you, you're waiting for everyone to show up. Wonderful. I'm not too much. I'll give them the whole party."

The country mouse said to me, "But if monsieur doesn't love you anymore, and if he loves me—"

"I don't know you, mademoiselle."

"I'm a madame."

"That's too bad for you. I'm not talking to you. I wouldn't want to say anything nasty to you. But since you don't know much about the world—which I find surprising at your age—you should know that even when he doesn't love me, he still can't be in love with you. After a great passion, the heart needs a break. You could be a million times prettier and you still wouldn't take my place. You hardly know him; you can't love him."

She began to cry because my words were confirmed by Robert's silence.

"All right," I said to him, "I don't want to kick madame out at this hour. You are going to come with me; she can leave at daybreak."

He saw that there was no other option to take without causing injury or scandal, and he agreed.

He said some kind words to console her, made excuses for his weakness, and vowed to her that if he had met her sooner he would have adored her, but his feelings couldn't be pushed aside.

He ordered his servant to tell all his friends that the party was rescheduled for the next week.

We went back to my place in silence.

He played the victim, boasted to me about her, and said, "I only came along with you to prevent a ridiculous scene."

That was fine with me. I didn't feel anything in my heart but my willpower. He was beside me in any case.

My cold, distant demeanor—despite the traces of a deep depression that were still on my face—changed his mind little by little. He came around completely, asked for my forgiveness, and assured me that he'd never stopped loving me for even an hour.

The next day, that woman wrote to him at my house to ask him for more money. He finally sent it to her to get it over with.

We went back to the apartment, and I assured myself that she was gone. The apartment was empty. He couldn't help but laugh. She'd wanted a souvenir and had taken an enormous pâté de foie gras.

41

IN PARIS, ANYTHING THAT COULD keep the masses entertained was enormously popular. I was gawked at twenty times whenever I did the promenades, and everyone wanted to see my rival. She was pretty, and she referred to herself as a victim of Robert's con. She was married and had several children in the country. She made herself more intriguing, and she found a huge audience among the curious and those who wanted to console her. She lost no time in becoming—like me—one of those pathetic celebrities, one of those women who devour both fame and the future. She was so thankful to all of her fans that I was surprised by the size of her gratitude. You could never say she didn't have heart. She deeply involved with about twenty people, to my knowledge.

Her crushes were her weakness. Everyone was happy.

I thought I myself had achieved a higher level of notoriety. I was mistaken. I still had room to climb, a new world to see.

Robert had me over a week later. I was the guest of honor at the party. They were very pleasant to me. My victory over that country mouse was talked about, like the fact that she wanted a carriage like mine. All this annoyed me because, in spite of myself, I was jealous. I hated her, and I made a show of my happiness so that she would envy me.

We gambled, and Robert lost. He didn't have a stroke of luck the entire night. Everyone who took his money laughed and said, "You can't have all the luck. When you have two women who love you, it proves the old saying: Unlucky in gambling, unlucky in love." He was a good sport, but I saw an almost imperceptible bead of sweat form on his brow. I took note of it.

"Well," I said to him, "you can leave the table!" I smiled at him pleasantly because I knew his problem, and I knew that the next day, he would regret not having listened to me.

By the time the party ended, he had lost eighteen thousand francs.

He went out early the next morning to try to raise some money. His assets were tied up, and he could only find lenders who asked 25 percent interest. When he came back, he said to me, "I don't know what to do. I need this money tonight; I owe people."

I had a moment of wicked joy in thinking that he would owe me. I made him an offer, which did not come at all from the goodness of my heart.

"You know," I said, "that my grandfather is rich. He

owned a hotel for twenty-five years. The government bought it off him, and he got a lot of money. If you want, I'll loan you, through him, twenty thousand francs. This will cost you nothing, or very little."

He accepted.

I came back about a half hour later and handed him twenty thousand francs in Spanish notes.

"Pay everyone," I said. "This is a loan to give you time to find the money at more reasonable rates."

He promised to repay me by the end of the week.

He had people over once a week. Whether he was hoping to make up his losses or just wanted a distraction, he kept gambling and losing.

In the smaller bedroom of his apartment, he had a jewelry box with many compartments. In the largest, there were drawers made to hold twenty thousand francs in gold coins. Robert had received ten thousand francs from his estate, which he deposited in this jewelry box. He had put a purse made of steel beads next to it, inside of which he had put all sorts of gold and foreign coins in larger denominations. He probably had about eight hundred francs in there. I regarded all of this with worry because I had a premonition that he would lose it.

He'd invited more guests than was usual, including some women to keep me occupied: Hermance, Brochet, P. M. ..., and a short woman that one of his friends brought along. She had a beautiful voice, and she was destined for the theater as a student of Duprez. Her face was stern, but she was friendly and covered me with kisses. Since she'd arrived first, she came into the dressing room to help me. She never gambled the whole night. Near two o'clock in the morning, after supper, she excused herself from the table, and no one minded.

At five o'clock, everyone left. Robert went to open his money box to pay out. The key to this box was attached to the chain of the mantel clock above the fireplace, and the glass was shatterproof. He took out a few thousand francs, paid his friends, and once he was alone, counted the money.

I had fallen asleep on a sofa. He awoke me and said, "You took the purse."

"Moi! Non, you know perfectly well that I don't gamble."

We looked everywhere. We got lost in our theories. One single person remained: Robert could not suspect the people he had invited. He considered the servants. Suspicion is an awful state of mind, and he'd have to see these people again or cut himself off from society. So I had an idea.

"Listen," I said, "when I got back from London, Maria came to see me. She also wanted to find out something, and she asked me to go the house of a somnambulist. I took her to Alexis Didier's. I didn't believe in clairvoyance at all, and I wanted to make a liar out of him anyway. I told myself, If he correctly answers the question I'm going to ask him, I'll believe him. We went. It was a public séance. Everyone was there. I gave him a lock of hair, took his hand, and asked him where the person whose hair I'd handed him was. Is he in France? Is he doing well?

"Alexis laughed and said, 'You say "he," but it's "she" we're talking about. This is the hair of a woman, and she is doing very well. She's here. It's you.'

"I looked around, unsettled. But I wanted more proof, so I said, 'You're wrong.'

"'Non,' he said, laughing even harder, 'it's not a bad

idea, what you've done. You come into a dim room, you light a candle, you wait over to the side, you close the door so that you can't be seen, you cut a lock of your hair into short pieces, and here they are.'

"I was blown away by what he said. This was the precise truth. I was scared of this mysterious power that can read thoughts. Maria saw me turn so pale, become so moved, that she didn't dare interrogate him further, thinking that you don't say anything to him that you don't want others to hear.

"'I'll come back when he's alone,' she said, and we left.

"It took a long time for me to pull myself together. I felt that he'd affected my mind, so I swore to never go back. But today, the case is very serious. If you want, we will consult him tomorrow morning to see if anyone knows about the theft."

My idea seemed sound. We found ourselves at Didier's, rue Grange-Batelière, with a friend of Robert's who would help at the séance.

As soon as Alexis was asleep, he was presented with the box, which had been locked with the key. He described the color and shape of the interior. He found the metal that had been handed to him hard to determine; however, he finally said, "There's gold at the bottom. You take it from inside."

"Oui," Robert said, "but someone else touched it. Look."

"Bring me to your house," Alexis said, gesturing that he would follow.

At Robert's, Alexis took stock of the apartment and said, "I see a woman who is dressing—they are two, wealthy. The one who is sitting is small, brunette; she's wearing a light-colored dress and a red ribbon around her neck. She's combing her hair, and she listens at the door. She takes something from the fireplace. It's a key. Oh! She's dropped it, something shatterproof. It's a mantel clock. She gets up, she opens your box, she takes without looking. It's not gold that she takes, it's gray. It's steel. Ah! I see, it's a purse. There are foreign coins inside, large coins. She doesn't put them in her pocketbook; she attaches the purse under her dress using a drawstring on her underskirt. She leaves the room, she goes toward the tall woman. She's not at all worried."

"Could you bring me to her?" Robert asked, amazed as I was at what we'd been told.

"Oui," Didier said. "Wait."

He walked around the living room as if it were the twisted streets of Paris, then said, "Here we are, rue B.... It's the second door on the left as you go in; she's on the fourth floor. Oh! But she's not there. There are women present, her mother and sister, and the dress from last night is on the bed."

"But her," Robert said, "do you see her? What did she do with the purse?"

"Hold on while I follow her. Wait, it's an actress— non, it's not a theater. There are a lot of people, and they're singing. She's about to leave."

We remembered her saying that she was studying at the conservatory.

"Come on," Robert said to me. "I'm going to her place. The money doesn't matter to me, but she has to give me back the purse. It was a gift from my mother."

We ran to rue B.... Alexis had described it perfectly. There were two women on the fourth floor who asked us to wait. The woman from the night before returned almost immediately and became livid as soon as she saw us. She was stubborn as a mule and indignantly denied that she'd taken the purse. Robert told her that if he didn't have his purse by the next day, he would have her arrested. She had brought this on herself. She wanted to sue us for one hundred thousand francs in damages.

She left Paris that night and didn't come back for years.

42

Robert lost most of the money he'd intended to pay me back. He made the rounds again. It was dinners and parties every day. I didn't say anything to him; I couldn't fight his spending anymore. I held it at arm's length or even encouraged it. When he bought some new extravagance, or when he bought me some expensive present, I didn't even say thank you. Dripping in his gifts and glowing with pride, I made myself the symbol of his ruin. I was the embodiment of the old saying, "Ingratitude is the heart's independence." I became a little notorious for it, which I'll allow I regretted once I realized it. I told myself that whatever Robert didn't give to me, he would give to that country mouse. With this kind of nonsense in her head, a jealous and poorly raised woman would drink all the tea and not leave a drop of water for the fish.

We had new friends. Mme. Rémi, a very elegant and capable woman, was Robert's neighbor. She invited us to spend the evening at her place. She had a handsome apartment, which was the greatest of her charms.

One day, Az… discouraged me from seeing her. Az… was a charming actress, daughter of an artist. She was raised backstage at a theater, but she didn't like theater women. Whenever the poor little thing said a word, they called her stupid. She was so nice! There are lots of people who are made stupid by calling them so; it kills any intellect that may have grown inside them. When Az… became a woman, she wanted revenge for what had been done to her as a child. She became very quarrelsome with everyone and only spoke to spread lies about her "dear sisters," as she called her colleagues in the theater. Myself, I studied her and knew she had a good heart. Her father had remarried, so she had stepsisters who had lost their mother. She replaced the mother to raise the little girls, whom she called her children. I saw the sacrifices she made for them, though she was only eighteen. This wasn't the reason she seemed older; it was her good heart.

About Mme. Rémi, she said to me, "Why do you go to her house? I don't like her myself; she's too lucky when she gambles. She used to throw gambling parties for women. She won everything, and when we ran out of money, she made us bet with whatever he had. She won my earrings, Brochet lost a very nice cashmere wrap, and Sarah lost the most to her. So everyone quit."

I was surprised she would tell me this. Before I would believe it, I checked with the others. Everyone said the same thing.

Robert threw a drag ball. It was wonderful and made me very happy, because it gave me an occasion to meet the little Page. There was something so sweet, so relaxed, in her big black eyes that they seemed like a mirror of her good and beautiful soul. I was also enchanted to see those great masters of drama up close: Mmes. Octave, Nathalie, etc. Nathalie was not very cheerful in those days! I cannot judge her for that. This particular day, her usual spirit had gone missing. She had come to try to forget a lost love, and since it was a literary passion, she showered the ball with her tears. At that point I had only seen Mme. Octave at the theater; this was during her huge success in *La Propriété c'est le Vol*. She was beautiful, and her personality matched her looks.

I watched all of these women with curiosity. I had only glimpsed them from afar; I found them even prettier up close. But it was above all the character of each that I wanted to know. They were all at least fifty years old.

I stopped in front of a charming woman from Breton, who turned out to be the little Durand. She had everything going for her: beauty, body. It didn't take her long once she'd noticed me to know this all too well and that I'd be less attractive in comparison.

I found myself face to face with a tall, beautiful person while dancing a quadrille. I searched my mind for where I'd seen her before. Afterward, I asked someone who it was, and I was told, "That's C…, an actress at Variétés."

Az… came up beside me. "She's pretty," I said to her.

"You think she's pretty, do you? She's dumb as a cabbage."

"You're so funny, my dear friend. Even if she were dumb, does that mean she can't have a pretty face?"

"You are so exhausting in your mania for picking out all the pretty women. I myself find them all ugly. Besides, if you only knew how they were lined up against you. I'm astonished to see them here."

"Come on, Az… Don't say that. Be fair, it's the only way to be true."

The dancing at the far end the salon stopped, and Robert went to open a window. Mlle. Page had become unwell; the heat was suffocating her. I took care of her. She thanked me and said as she took her leave, "It would be very kind of you to come see me."

I promised her I would.

"Poor Page!" said a short woman who I hadn't noticed before. "She's too tightly wound. That's what made her ill."

Good soul! I said to myself. This woman's false concern hid nastiness inside it.

"Will you come dance, Amanda?" said a tall, brown-haired man.

I stood behind her and watched her for a long time. She had a pretty face, though her nose was a little too long and her lips too thin. She was small and delicate and engulfed by tulle, though dressed artfully. Her arms were bare and her hands bony. Despite this, I was surprised when she called Mlle. C. "my sister." Nature had done so much for one and so little for the other. I had already figured, without knowing them, that one would envy the other.

These parties Robert threw were very expensive. He became depressed once we were alone, and he tried to drown his sorrows.

The next day, he asked that a coupe with eight springs be brought around and put me in it. I went to visit Page, who I'd made into a friend. I wasn't mistaken—she was a kind as she was pretty.

Time passed, and Robert didn't pay back the money that I'd loaned him. I began to worry, because I'd lose everything—along with him.

43

The Soul's Accountants—A Dinner with New Acquaintances

ROBERT HAD BUSINESS AT HIS estate and left for Berry for two days.

I was invited to the house of a fairly famous actress who was giving a dinner for all women guests. There were eight of us, but I won't say their names. Like me, maybe they'll write about those years of their lives. I don't have the right to call them out. I'll refer to them by the number of their places at the table.

We waited in a lovely salon next to the room where dinner would be served. The mistress of the house opened a double door, and we entered a dining room decorated with antique Chinese furniture, paintings, and curios on the enormous buffet. It looked like a shop—the abundance was there, the taste was not.

We said our hellos to each other. We put on airs as if we were great ladies to make up for having had to eat potatoes in our youth. I was only at their level on this last point—I had eaten as many potatoes as they had. But I didn't know how to sweeten my voice, to take a microscope to my demeanor. I had kept my real name, and I did not pose with one arm garlanded, my hands held as if cradling a butterfly.

I knew what these women would say: She lacks distinction. But I was me.

Dinner was served.

"Ladies," said our hostess, "I've marked your places."

Number 1: She was a tall, beautiful girl who seemed both sweet and stupid. Number 2 was small, thin, and pinched. Number 3 was a tall, little-known ingenue. Number 4 was a country girl, Number 5 a woman who must have been pretty ten years before. Number 6 was a kind and simple girl who only liked violet diamonds. I was Number 7, and Number 8 was the hostess, a pretty blonde who was fading with age.

The dinner came from Chez Potal and Chabot. There were two maître d's who embarrassed me a little because they seemed not to bother themselves with chitchat.

"Oh, my dear," said Number 2, "your dinner will be inedible, with the stoves being cold. At my house, we serve a la Russe. It's very good that way. I don't like this stew. Why didn't you have them make a bisque?"

"My dear," answered the hostess, "you forgot to send me your menu."

"Your silver is lovely," said Number 1, weighing a

spoon in her hand, "but I like mine better."

"You all are lucky. I only have a dozen place settings," grumbled Number 5. "I've tried to drop my lover a hint so they he'd let me buy more, but he hasn't picked it up."

"You yourself aren't picked up," said Number 2.

"I'd like to see you take it up with him," retorted Number 5. "I had to scheme for a month to get a dress."

"I believe it," Number 6 whispered to me. "He doesn't know how to take care of her. She's stayed with him for four years. She tells him that she's pregnant and she's going to kill herself, her and the child, if he leaves her."

"I tried a trick that was not all that stupid. I invited more of his friends to dinner, and the morning of the party said, 'My God, dear, I don't have enough place settings. If you would be so kind, let me buy them.' At four o'clock, he sent me a box. I was charmed, but that didn't last long. He was just loaning me his silver. I was out of luck. I do not know of a man more stubborn than this one."

"Lady," said Number 4, "you're the one being stubborn. He's very good to you. He gives you a thousand francs a month and lots of gifts."

"You're given two thousand, you are," Number 5 said tartly. "Do you think that I don't know what you're worth?"

"When it comes to my personality, no," said Number 4 with a laugh.

"Nor for my body anymore," Number 6 said to me. She was at least thirty.

"But," continued Number 5 after a pause, "I'm in the middle of preparing him for emotional blackmail. You know that he loves children. I think that if I have one, he'll marry me, even being the marquis that he is. Well! I'm going to get into bed and say that I'm sick. I found someone who will say that I'm pregnant. Then I'll cry and make such a big deal of it that he'll have to raise my income."

"It's not a bad plan, if works," said Number 8, "but be careful. He pretends to be dumber than he is."

"How could anyone want a baby?" said Number 4. "I am the unlucky woman who has one every year."

"Oui," said Number 2, looking at her, "but you have a way to keep them from inconveniencing you."

"Well, if I didn't make things right, I would be kind. I've had seven. I'm like the mère Gigogne."

My heart seized. This woman was notorious. She committed crimes to maintain her luxurious lifestyle. She removed these little beings from her life so as not to miss a party or a ball. Everyone knew about it. She was the preeminent mistress of many of the highest classes, of those who know perfectly well that they have a good name only to ruin it for fashion, to dirty it with vices, and without even true love as an excuse. Everyone laughed at every new revelation about this woman.

"Speaking of which," said Number 8, "I received a letter from Belgium. He's safe. I'm glad; he's a good boy."

"Did he give you all that?" asked Number 6.

"Oui," responded Number 8. "That's how much he loves me."

"You know how to pinch them," said Number 5.

"That why I discreetly studied the man, I did," answered Number 8 as she drained her glass of madeira.

The wine was excellent. The maître d's, who were amused by this conversation, stepped up to fill her glass with blazing red faces. They said no more than they absolutely had to.

As for myself, the new guest among these elegant women, what I heard made them all seem silly.

"I think," said Number 4, "that he had to be in love to find that money after going broke. In any case, it's lucky that he's left. He would have compromised you."

"I'm not in any danger," said Number 8 with a laugh. "If I had done it myself, fine. But I'm not that dumb!"

"What did he do?" I asked my neighbor.

"Oh, of course," said Number 5, "you don't know the story. I'll tell you." She came over to me and began speaking quietly.

THE HOSTESS'S STORY
She had a charming young man from a very good family as a lover. He didn't love her at first, but little by little he went crazy for her. She took him to fancy shops where she made him buy loads of things. Usually it was furniture or paintings that she had sent to her place. It seems that shopping this way became an obsession. She never asked him for money; however, he was broke within two years. She wanted to break it off, but he said he would kill himself.

But that's not why she stayed with him. She found a way to make it work: She threw gambling parties, they ate well, there were a lot of society people, and they played cards. She stationed herself next to him, and he played his hand after her. He lasted ten or eleven rounds with each hand. Everyone around him cheered him on. She never gambled with her own money, and people lost ridiculous sums. However, she always made a case for playing for higher stakes. She bought a carriage and horses and took unmatched care of the way she earned her wealth. This went on with heedless happiness. If he hadn't been a man with a position, he would have been taken for a cheat.

He had already won more than two hundred thousand francs when a gentleman who had lost a lot noticed that every night the hostess left the table to put on a dressing gown. This gentleman became suspicious because she never changed seats. She said, "I want to be near *my boyfriend*. I bring him luck." So this gentleman sat himself between them and, while making small talk, passed his hands over both their purses. In hers, he could feel a deck of cards.

"What do you have there?" he said, squeezing the cards through the pocket of her dressing gown and looking her in the face. Despite his cool, she became livid, and everyone could see it.

"Me?" she said. "These are unlucky cards that I removed from the deck when they didn't help."

"Oh?" The gentleman smiled in a way that did not bode well. "Show them to me."

She quickly pulled them from her pocket and dropped them on the floor, where they scattered. Everyone murmured without daring to speak aloud, but everyone was sure they'd been cheated.

Her lover, who didn't suspect a thing, said, "Are we not playing anymore?"

Everyone took their cue and picked up their hats. He was surprised that she'd been passing him the cards. They assured everyone that he didn't know they were stacked. Since this little episode made a lot of noise, she sent him to Brussels to work in trade.

"I remember hearing this story," I said.

Other conversations had been taken up, but Number 8, the woman in question, had heard us. She said to Number 6, "My dear, you have a terrible fault: always sharing the stories of others and never your own. I have beautiful furniture, you have beautiful jewelry, but neither of us is worth anything. Let's try not to throw stones at each other, since we're the only people who will defend us."

I wanted to know Number 6's story, so I said to Number 8, "Is it true, what she told me?"

"Non," she said, "*no one can prove it*. But what is certain and proven is that she charges these poor people interest. She lends by the week at the hall. When her lovers need money, she tells them, 'I know someone who can loan it to you.' 'Someone' is her brother. He shows up and says, 'I don't have any money at the moment, but I'm about to buy some gorgeous diamonds. If you want, I'll sell those to you.' Having no better option, they take the diamonds. The lovers sign the letters of exchange, she keeps it all—the money and the diamonds—and the circle is closed. Even at this very moment, she's got one guy in Clichy, and she's worked out a deal with the parents of another."

"It's so funny that you talk about it like that," said Number 2 as she stood up. "What does it matter? When it works, it's all good."

"Certainly," said Number 1. "Me, I stood to make sixty thousand francs off of mine. His father was about to kick the bucket, and I was ready to lock him in a cage if he didn't pay me. But no luck. The old man held on to his life like bark on a tree. Every day, I made sure to get news of his health. If I'd been sure nothing would happen to me, I would have given him a little nudge along his way." We all laughed.

Number 1 hadn't shared any great stories, so Number 2 said, "Tell your story about the Hungarian."

"You want it," she said calmly, "fine. Imagine, ladies: All the women were running after him because he was very rich. But he didn't keep any of them around. I told myself, 'There has to be at least one woman who captivates him.' I asked his valet, who told me, 'Monsieur is devout. He's always at mass.' I went to mass many times, and he saw me nearby. He told me that I was an angel dropped among you, which raised me up in his esteem. But the idea of going back to the church again bored me, because my feet got cold. By the way," she said to Number 3, "how's it going with your married man?"

"Fine."

"What? What?" said all the women in a chorus.

"I was with someone who was so determined to be mysterious," said Number 3, "that he wore me out. I ended up learning that he was married, but his wife wasn't in Paris. I told him that I wanted to go to a fancy ball, and I wanted to wear diamond earrings. He pleaded poverty, but I told him that I wanted the earrings or I would never see him again. 'Fine,' he said, 'I can't buy them, but since it's for a ball, I can loan them to you.' He brought me dazzling earrings, which were his wife's. I took them to my jeweler, and I had him take out the diamonds and put glass in their place. I returned them to him, and he didn't even notice. After a few days, his wife returned to Paris. I asked him again if he would buy me earrings, and he refused. So I made a huge scene. 'Your wife has diamonds, and you don't want to give me any, eh? Then I'm happy with what I've done. Just for laughs, I kept them. I have the diamonds, and she has glass.' He jumped back, groaned, begged, threatened, and became furious."

"You have no fear," said Number 2.

"Non, I knew that he wouldn't do anything for fear of scandal."

"Well played," said the others. "You have a quiet strength."

It was midnight, so I left along with Number 6. As we went out, she said, "I don't want to see anyone anymore. I like living alone better. They're too mean, and a good girl like me gets lost in their midst. For me, under the influence of a short, bright moment, I considered them all great men."

Back at my place, I fell asleep, exhausted by all I'd heard. The worst thoughts pressed into my mind, like the worst weeds in a wheat field. If you don't pull them, they spread and kill the crop, the best parts of the soul. You can always take one step farther along the path of evil. My soul was too poorly tended for bad advice to take root very quickly. My brain was working, because I also wanted to have a story to tell the next time I found myself with these women. Oh, I thought, I've proven myself too: Deligny is in Africa, Richard in California, and Robert is out of the picture.

I could see these wretched women—and myself—tied to the pillory in public yet laughing at their notoriety, as long as they're being talked about. Others nearby weep and try to hide their faces. They've committed the same crimes, and they've submitted to the same punishment. One causes horror in the viewer, the other pity. If I had examined my past life and personality, I would have seen that during this time I took part in shameful vices, but I only hurt myself. What these women were doing was brazen corruption. Everyone could see it, and the accomplices of the moment had no fear for the future. My new lifestyle was less vilified by society. It's an injustice. That which we call woman is the user of the heart and the usurer of the soul.

Men, who created this squadron from hell, are proud of their work and put these demons on a pedestal. On foot, you wouldn't see them. They're given magnificent horses and carriages, passing their mothers and sisters along the promenade. Some of them are driven by their weaknesses, and they toss a defiant glance toward honest women. These creatures are ignoble, and their creators are infamous. Their souls are damned for good, but the pain of retribution awaits them. These apartments, which they've made so beautiful, are the tombs of their wealth. They leave everything there: youth, the future, honor. In a moment of need, the lace curtains turn into shrouds, the roses into marigolds, and the perfumes into poison.

Then, the unlucky one who traipsed into this pit cries out. Her mistress appears, but she's a zombie. God took away the life he had given her. The devil gave her speech and movement, and she can no longer think. It's he who moves her, and she says to her weeping lover, "Why are you still here? Get out."

The condemned man begs, reminds her what he has done for her, what he sacrificed.

"Why did you do all that?" she asks.

"Because I loved you!"

"Well, then," says the mistress as she stretches, "I shouldn't feel bad for you for sacrificing yourself. However, you have nothing more to give, so off you go."

He sees everything clearly then. He would take her back, she's his idol, but she tramples him under her horses' hooves.

Those who come to this end are pushed by pride, and it's pride that punishes them. These women don't stop.

They don't notice the wrinkle on their forehead. They end up in the hospital, the prison, or the morgue. They'll get their punishment in the future, but their passage has left a terrible scar on society.

What would I do with all of these reflections? Ever since the day I tried to kill myself at Robert's, the demon had possessed me. I became mechanical, ungrateful, and I found an excuse for everything I did. Soon enough I took on the sad celebrity status of a dangerous woman. I was shamed less when I danced and called myself Mogador. Now if a young man sought me out or spoke to me, his parents made him leave me alone. I was proud to inspire such terror.

44

A Madness, a Mistake

I was at Robert's. He had come back. He'd grown bored with his estate, he couldn't raise any money, and his depression made his worries obvious.

He tried to sell his land, because he had borrowed just under three hundred thousand francs against it. Although it was priced at eight hundred thousand francs, the interest ate up the revenue. There was an offer at six hundred thousand francs, but he refused it. I begged him to pay me back for covering his gambling debts. He couldn't do it.

One day, seeing that I was thoughtful, he asked what I was doing.

"I'm thinking of the future. I wanted to ask you something, but I'm afraid of upsetting you."

"Me? Why the devil should something upset me?"

"Because I know that you don't have any cash and that it's not right to ask you for any."

"Well!" he said with his usual haughty pride. "I'll raise it, if I don't have it. How much do you need?"

"I only want what you owe me, or a guarantee of payment if anything happens to you. Everyone is mortal. I would lose everything I have."

"Hold on—that money came from you?"

"Oui."

"Why did you trick me into letting you give it to me?" he said, turning pale as death.

"Because you wouldn't have accepted it if I'd said it was mine."

"Oh, Céleste, what you've done is awful. You've made me an accomplice in a shameful deed. That money came from you…" He didn't finish. A fat tear rolled down his cheek. "If I had known…" he said, getting up from his seat. "I can't pay you back immediately; the land has to sell. Tomorrow I'll try. I'll go to my accountant."

His attempts were useless, and he became deeply depressed.

After dinner, I asked if he wanted to go out.

"Non," he said, "we have to talk. You're right to think of the future, but I am distraught at having taken this money. You've done yourself harm. I must repay you as soon as possible. Now that I know where it came from, I can't stand it. Breaking up with you will make me miserable, but that's how it has to be. I'm going to get married; if I don't, this will haunt me for the rest of my life, even if my land sells. I can't give you a promissory note from my notary; my family knows him. They would think I was giving you a gift, and they'll yell about it. That would shut down my plans. Here's what I propose. I'm going to give you letters of exchange, and I'll pay you for them as soon as I can. If I haven't paid in full by the date on the notes, you'll take me to court and I'll consent to terms. I must leave town in a few days; I have to take a quick trip to Lyon. I can't keep this apartment. Tomorrow we'll go to the owner, and I'll ask him to take you on as a renter in my place. I hope he doesn't say no. You'll stay here, if you like it here."

"And my place," I said, "what am I going to do with it?" In order to be closer to him, I had rented a place in a small building on rue Joubert—very nice, but a little pathetic.

"Rent it out."

Two days later, the lease was in my name.

⁂

My mother had been ill, and she was alone. She came to see me fairly often. I was afraid of giving myself over to some new weakness. I put my money in my mother's hands, telling her not to pay anyone under any pretext. This was my savings for my adopted daughter.

I was able to rent out my apartment and sell all my furniture. It broke my heart to sell the wonderful tapestries that reminded me of my time in Berry. Mlle. Amanda wanted to buy my furnishings, since she'd always envied them.

Robert wanted me to accept all offers. He gave me one reason then another, but the real motive was that everything I had gotten from Richard bothered him. Pushed by this person, pestered by that one, I sold everything in this little apartment for twenty thousand francs. It was charmingly furnished, carpets in all the rooms, chestnut and rosewood furniture, piano, organ, draperies—everything.

I would be paid for it all in three years.

Robert left town.

I saw everything I did and everything in the room through the lens of his absence. But he was leaving me to get married. Maybe I would never see him again. I went a few days without giving him a second thought. I went to this friend's house, to that friend's. The time flew like a dream.

One of my new acquaintances, who I'd brought back to my place, saw a picture of my goddaughter.

"It's wonderful that you have a plant to sow," she said. "She'll be pretty, and she must be a dancer. She'll earn money, and you'll get a cut."

I felt a shiver pass over me. I saw her mother in my mind, and she repeated to me the promise I had made. "Non, I'll never make her a dancer. She'll be rich, but if I had to give her a position in society, it would not be that."

"Oh!" she said, laughing. "Are you afraid of a little faux pas?"

One day, I stopped at place de la Madeleine and went up to Mlle. Page's. I had just broken up with my other friends. The cynical things that they said about my adopted daughter had thrown me for a loop. They thought I was raising her to pimp her out. The thought made me so sick I couldn't hold back my tears.

Poor little Page couldn't pick me up with her own cheerfulness. She felt terrible herself; her life was dominated by a great love affair that ate at her physically and morally. She was emaciated, her cheeks were pale, but her eyes were still shining—because they were full of tears. She was unlucky in everything. She had a little girl that she'd watched waste away and die. The art of medicine was powerless. The poor little chest of this child always rattled. Death came on slow steps, as if to draw out the destruction of her mother's heart. Often, when I was dining at her place, I saw her drop her bread, look at her daughter in rapture, then begin to weep without moving a muscle. She looked like a beautiful statue in mourning. My heart shared her pain, and I became close as a sister to her.

These were not her only troubles; she was so pretty, so adorable, and her voice was so sweet as a woman and as an actress, that the public adored her. Her colleagues in the theater were jealous of her, who you couldn't imagine saying a mean word. Page's health was fragile, and I was afraid she would fall ill.

To be nearer to her, I had an idea. I was alone, and I knew Robert was not coming back. *This will take my mind off things*, I said to myself. So I asked Page to get me an audition at Variétés.

She introduced me to M. C..., the producer. He promised to hire me. I wrote to him that I would like it to be a done deal as soon as possible. He had me return to his office. He was not handsome enough for me to bother painting a portrait for you. That day he didn't seem too clumsy. He had me sign a contract giving me 1,200-franc salary with a 20,000-franc kill fee.

These girls raised a ruckus at my being hired.

For poor Page, this was a new source of tension that she wasn't prepared for, since she only knew me to be a true friend.

I was given roles in the *Revue de Cinquante et Un*. I was a regular by the time Robert came back from Lyon.

"Well," he said, "I couldn't get married. I was turned down every time because of you. I no longer have any choice in the matter. I'm going to sell my horses, my dogs, renovate most of my house, and we'll stay together."

"But, my friend, I can't leave with you. I didn't think you were coming back, so I returned to the theater. I have a salary and a recurring role. It's a good plan to sell all those things. I can't keep the house up myself. Sell your smaller carriage, the large coupe that you gave me with two horses, and later on I'll sell my little coupe and carriage."

He seemed firmly against my engagement at the theater, but he didn't say anything about it to me. He sold his horses, his carriages, and only stayed in Paris for a short while.

Amanda asked me if I wanted to sell some jewelry, since I had so much that I should be disgusted. I told her that one can't be disgusted by such things, that I was sane enough to unload some of it if I found the right time.

"Great," she said, "you'll never find better. You'll get paid in full for your furniture in three years. Consider the capital that these could provide you."

I was twenty-five years old, and I wanted my goddaughter to be rich. I consented. I sold the matching sets for a little less than their retail price, but it was as if I'd made three years of interest. Page approved.

⁂

One evening, Robert said to me, "I ran into a young man that I knew. The poor boy made me depressed. He's at his wits' end because they're going to arrest him. I could maybe prevent it, because it's my jeweler who's after him. I asked him."

"Be careful," I said. "You'll have some dirty business

on your hands. You know my opinion of your jeweler. He's a fine fox. Watch yourself."

Alas! He didn't take my advice at all. A few days later, everything had been swallowed up. Robert had underwritten a sum of twenty thousand francs for a man who was insolvent. I grumbled at him for a week. He told me that this poor young man wanted to kill himself.

"In the end," I said, "whatever he may be, you were played."

Robert left for the country, and I asked him to check on my little house. I wanted to build a pavilion on the side. Because it was located near the woods, Robert asked me to construct a hunting lodge, which I could rent at a good price until the time came that I wanted to move in. I told him that I'd leave it completely up to him, and that anything he did would be fine.

He left, and I debuted onstage. I was always depressed. I had more stage fright than at the Folies. Page encouraged me, and she gave me such good advice that I could only benefit from it. The papers took pains to bring me down. They said my footwork was like an old woman's. At last, at the ripe old age of twenty-five, they were sending me to les Invalides. Some people imposed themselves on me; the smaller they were, the less likely it was that they were regulars, and the nastier they were. If they didn't have season tickets, they tore you down. Not even Arnal and Déjazet were safe from their attacks. It's a heavy burden for the poor artists who earn their living from pain and who are obliged to subscribe to three or four papers that all say the same thing. The paper *Le Corsair*, this snarling dog of literature, bled me to death.

Those who most freely went after me also attacked the plays themselves. I consoled myself by saying, "He's a worse playwright than I am a bad actress, because they're hissing at him, they're not hissing at me."

I was about to be in a new piece, *Paris Qui Dart*. M. C... said to me, "You absolutely must go see M. J.... He does not like your acting."

"Damn it! What do you want me to do? If he doesn't like me, I can't force him to change his taste."

"You have to go for the sake of the act," he said. "He'll see you."

"I doubt it," I said. "I don't dare."

"Oui, oui," said M. C.... "Do it for me."

"Fine, to make you happy, I'll go."

I went to Amanda's that same day. She knew him well; she was always in his box opening night. I asked her to introduce me to her friend. But I'd forgotten that I pushed myself on her, and from that day on, she couldn't stand me. That's just how it was. She wouldn't do anything for me, or she'd do the opposite of what I asked.

I went to M. J...'s. My heart was thumping out of my chest after climbing five flights of stairs, plus I was scared to death at the idea of finding myself face to face with such a great writer. I was shown in while he was speaking to his parakeet, with whom he continued the conversation.

I was thrown for a loop, and it took all my effort to say, "Monsieur, I know that you're prejudiced against me. My past, in your opinion, condemns me. However, I want to do serious work in the theater. Your judgement carries so much weight, I want to ask you to not speak ill of me. Later, if I succeed on the strength of my work, I'll be grateful that you didn't crush me as I was starting out."

"Mademoiselle," he said, "I am sorry, but my review is already in. Besides, I wouldn't explain my words: *You have to be tricky to grasp them*, as you say in your role."

"But, monsieur, I didn't write it." His frosty demeanor stunned me, and I felt tears roll down my cheeks.

No doubt he thought I was a silly girl, but he did make the edits to his review. I had escaped by the skin of my teeth.

Victorine came to see me the next day. "My dear," she said, "you've plunged yourself into hell. When you have to live among journalists, playwrights, actors, you might as well lodge yourself in the kennels at the Barriere du Combat. It would be less deadly, less destructive."

"Do you know Vervenne, who was at Vaudeville for a bit when she was fifteen? She told me the other day that she'd been hired at Variétés. I put in a good word for you there. If she's ever mean to you, which is bound to happen, ask her to show everyone her legs, and you'll have your revenge. One day I went to see her, and I had to wait an hour. I was about to leave when her maid said to me mysteriously, 'Wait another five minutes. Madame has finished drying.' 'Wait, what?' I said. 'Drying?' 'Oui, madame puts a white mask on her face, then it has to dry.'"

Since I had returned to the theater, Robert had been in Paris many times. He tried in vain to get me back.

Life in the theater was a distraction for me, but it didn't make me forget even a little bit.

When he saw that I absolutely did not want to get back together with him, he took his land in disgust and put it up for sale. He wrote me letter after letter. They were in turn tender and kind, then nasty and brutal. They bothered me to the point that I asked him a thousand times not to write me anymore. Then he resorted to begging, including weeping and wailing. Despite my not being involved with him anymore, I still found in my memories of our past a few kind words to give him courage and gently bring him to terms with our breakup.

To be brave, my dear Robert, you have to let this go. There are too many things between us for us to be happy from now on. You must think of your fortune, your future. This separation hurts me, but it's necessary to put on a good face for everyone who says you're causing your own downfall. Don't give jealous people anything to be happy about. I'm only your friend now. I only want your happiness.
Céleste

He wrote back:

I don't need your advice or your opinions. I'm no longer rich enough, so you don't want to see me anymore. Fine! You'll not hear another word from me.

Six hours later, I received another letter.

❦

I received an invitation to a ball that M. Philoxene, a playwright, was giving on New Year's Eve. I didn't want to go, but all my friends told me to come, that it would be fun, that there would be lots of artists there.

I put on a dress with a low-cut neckline and the jewelry I still had. A friend sent me a corsage, which I accepted so as not to be rude and embarrass myself.

When I entered the salon, I was very disappointed. There were all lot of guests, including all the actresses from Délassements-Comiques and Folies-Dramatiques.

They were all dressed in city garb—that is to say, revealing dresses. Everyone regarded me as a curiosity. I wasn't bothered by it anymore. There was only one place left to sit, so I asked a gentleman to escort me to it, promising myself that I wouldn't move an inch from that spot all evening.

On the same sofa was a woman in a red dress. I didn't look at her as I arranged myself next to her. She stood and all but jumped away from me, as if I'd burned her.

Everyone was watching her. I recognized her as Mlle. Judith, and I grew as red as her dress.

All these gentlemen crowded around me to defend me from this snub. This is how I had the pleasure of meeting M. Henri Murger, and I began to think better of my neighbor who had left her seat. I won in the end. Her friends chastised her for being so rude, and she balked at them.

Toward the end of the evening, M. Murger wrote a couplet for each of the guests who remained and put them in his hat. He then set these couplets to the tune of a song from *Quidant*:

There were twenty social climbers in the gallery

He avenged me by writing:

To vex the actress
Who wore imitation jewels,
Céleste, who chose her godmother
Long ago in Morocco,
Approached a snooty princess
In a blooming garden.
In Philoxene's salon,

We were eighty social climbers.

In the marble of her shoulders,
Golconde inlaid jewels,
Visapour bedazzled her hands,
You might say like a polar night sky.

In seeing all this splendor,
Judith balks at Holofernes.
In Philoxene's salon,
We were eight social climbers.

I was very proud that the author of *Bonhomme Jadis*, from *The Life of Boheme*, had for even a second let his pencil and his thoughts turn toward me. He had, within an hour, made forty couplets about his friends. I had two—too friendly, maybe.

The disdain of the pretty Jew had brought me luck.

※

I was about to appear in a new show when I received this letter from Robert:

Céleste, I cannot live like this. I counted too much on my courage. I can't live without you. Listen to what I propose. If you ever loved me, it lasted as long as a false flame, a spark, a dream, a party. Everything went up in flames, and I am destroyed. I have a recurring nightmare that follows me around. I wake up in a sweat, and I think I hear you singing gaily at the gambling table, in the midst of people who only want without love. They say to you, "I love you! I love you!" Do you know how much I love

you? It's madness! I am crazy. I offer you more than my wealth, I offer you my life, my name, my honor. I am going to liquidate my possessions. I'm selling my land in a few days. We'll be happy far away from here. Don't say no—I've thought a lot about it. I'll never have a single regret if you'll make my happy. Answer me quickly.
  Robert

I couldn't believe my eyes. I read the letter twenty times. I was so stunned I couldn't respond at first. My sense of self-preservation called out to me: "Say yes!" My heart wrote the following letter:

My dear Robert, I'm returning your letter, which could not possibly have been meant for a woman like me. Depression and loneliness have made you lose your mind. You'll have many regrets when the fever that's driving you breaks. I could come along with you in your life of lavish spending, though that would only drain your fortune. But to take away your honor, your good name. Ah, my friend! Burn this letter. It's written by a madman.

  Forget me. I've always told you I would never marry. Back then you said to me, laughing, "Not even to me?" and I answered, "Even less to you than to another, Robert, because of my past and your violent tendencies. Your count's crown would be a crown of thorns for me. I would no longer be able to see the poor pariahs I grew up with, yet I'd never have the status to look an honest woman in the eye."

  One mean word from you, and I'd kill myself. I told you this four years ago, and I'm saying it again now. You'll thank me later. There are two paths: yours and mine. Let me be Mogador, and you remain Robert de .... Leave this

drama behind. You'll be able to forget with a little courage. I'll always be your friend.
    Céleste

45

Leaving

I didn't keep any secrets from Page. I told her what I'd decided to do.

"Maybe you're wrong," she said.

"Non. He's made me pay dearly for his weakness. All the fights that I had with him plucked the petals from my love. I didn't make him happy. I'm going to the theater, and I'll stay there. I'm going to work hard. I'll only be happy the day I can live independently. I'll have some money, but it'll take me a few years to build up. I hope Robert decides to travel. He's going to sell off his assets. I'm afraid he's fooling himself; in the end, he'll stay here for his parents' wealth. He'll never be without. On the other hand, there's me. What would be on my horizon? Suicide!"

Six days later, I received a letter from Robert. It was

long, terrible, and hit me in a way that took me a long time get over.

Madwoman! Anyone who thinks that because they've given everything, they'll be remembered is kidding themselves. What they get in exchange is advice and pity. They say to you: So sorry to make you suffer. Forget me, be brave, try to make it all better. Here's a memory to keep. And then the letter ends, the deed is done, they laugh, and they take new lovers. The poor idiot bows his head without complaint because complaining shows a lack of courage.

I had everything—money, youth—and I threw it all to the wind. The only thing I still have to offer you is my name, but it's too little. Shame on me! I sacrificed everything for you, and you just put me down for my weakness. I was stupid, wasn't I, to want to make you a woman with a heart? I hoped for a note from you, but you didn't write. You don't even have the audacity to lie to me in a letter.

You are rotten to the core! You who I wrapped in my care to make you forget your name, you whose past I offered to forget. I gifted you a house! I can see you laughing from here. Your heart can't comprehend a woman having emotions. Your prediction will come true: You've left me with my last sou. I'm learning that I am indeed broke. I gave a businessman power of attorney to sell my estate in my absence. He took advantage of my trust and sold my land for half its value. How much did he get? It hardly matters; for me, it's all lost.

I'm going to leave and only come back when, exhausted, ashamed of the lowly tributes that you wanted and that you sacrificed for me, you call me back to you. I'll try to make you forget the blots on your heart. Go, Céleste, so that all my tears can again fall like a rain of fire over your existence. I loved you as you'd love an angel. God is punishing me, but I'm leaving you without hatred. All that's left to me is a poor and lonely life, which I brought on myself. My brain is bombarded by images of your dress for the theater and your bed of pleasure. When I sold my assets, I had to take my papers and portraits of my family to your little house. Sell them, because any memories will only bring me regret. I will not go to Paris; I do not want to give you the satisfaction of witnessing my moral and physical downfall.

I offered you my name. I never saw you as my mistress. You could be my north star, but you never considered me dignified enough for you. I was insane to believe in warm feelings from you, which in you were damaged the day you came into the world. On the tenth, I'm leaving for Africa.

I want to forget, because the memories are mine to kill. You should go to Russia. Women are happy there! There's little love and lots of money! Your theater should be able to advertise your actions. They'll say, "That's Céleste Mogador! Her Robert is broke, so he left for Africa." I gave you a good coat of arms for your carriage. Now it's a warning for all who see it.

The passion I have for you is a mystery to everyone, and to me. To love, you must have discernment, and I was wrong about you. This letter has gone on too long. This is the last thing I'll say, the swan song, because for the life of me it's over. It's right to allow a dying man a backward glance. I was born to be loved because I have a tender, loving heart. I need to be loved, but now my heart is broken and my life is finished. More than my friends, more than my parties, I'm going far away from myself. I hope to find death there and overcome it, to find in my own eyes an esteem that no one else holds me in any longer. The world is harsh, but it is fair. I'll try to become an honest man, and my past will be forgiven.

As for you, may your life of pleasure last a long time. Try not to let the night become morning, because waking up will be horrible. Then you'll know abandonment. You'll have nothing left but misery, this hideous hag! This child you're raising will look down on you. You'll see that the nights are long when you spend them crying. Do not write me ever again.

Robert

Never could I express how hurt I was on reading this letter. I spent hours in tears. My heart was destroyed, thrown to the ground. It took a massive effort for me to respond.

I am very hurt, my dear Robert, yet I must endure all your abuse. Pity me. For two days, your letters were depressing but kind. Today, you take me down for no reason.

The first day I met you, I told you who I was. You said that I didn't love you, when you know perfectly well that the opposite is true. And then, when you would cause me pain and make me cry due to your coldness or telling some truth that mortally wounds me, then you would come to soothe me with kind words and kisses. I rebelled, and every day drew away little by little from this love that still had a hold on my life.

I saw you buy expensive things for horses and dogs. I was jealous of the pleasure they gave you. You would tell me that you had to do this because you were hunting, but I didn't have the strength for it. I was being driven mad by a pleasure that you preferred to me, or so it seemed.

My ambition was always modest, and I often said to you, "If one day I had 1,200 francs in cash, I'd be able to erase my name from the books as a courtesan." You filled my life with gifts, I went about in a carriage with you, I lived like a queen. Yet when I told you I was afraid of the future, you answered that one of your mother's former servants was happy with her six-hundred-franc pension. But she has never known the vices that you put on our heart. A person can forget what they were, most of all when they find blame and misery in their memories. Myself, I never forgot the prison where I went, Saint-Lazare, where I would have stayed, because if I left I would have died of hunger. Where I saw the sick old women who flaunted once having had youth and beauty and who committed a crime in the street and were arrested because they didn't have bread or a place to stay. I never forgot that, and I never will. I wanted to write another ending for myself.

I loved your indulgences, and I predicted your ruin. I wanted to see you get married. I resigned myself to this separation for the sake of your happiness, but the idea never occurred to me that you'd take another mistress. You could have saved everything by getting married. I got from elsewhere what I didn't want from you and never asked of you. I could not bear the depression of knowing you were with another. I paid dearly for coming back to you with the little that I had. I put it at your disposal when I wanted to give you my life.

As time went on, worry overwhelmed me, and I asked you to repay me. This was unkind, but I was scared. This fear ate at me constantly. I had everything invested in hope and nothing in reality. Nights tormented me, and during the day I hid my worry under luxury. This woman that you'd taken up with, I fought for my self-esteem with her. I told myself this above all: Jewels, lace, carriages, I wanted them all. Sorry, this is not to pick a fight with you. Non, I loved you. Your lover released a fury in me. Today I would give my life to fix the past. I'm as afraid of being alone as you are of being married. Destiny is written; you can't steer it, you can only follow it.

I think that you could do something else for me. Your accusations are so exaggerated that I reexamined my life with you, and I found a little grace for myself in the fact that I never lied to you. You wanted me to start my life anew by giving me your name. Today I'd be notorious if I'd accepted your proposal; however, I had a sense that I'd not be able to fill this sacred role. Boredom, this shadow of ourselves, is always creeping up on me. I'm not young anymore, and I've lost my sense of joy. I work in the theater because I don't want anyone to be pleased we broke up. If I had my own small income, I would give up the life of luxury that hides so many tears. I would get used to a modest life that I could live out to the end.

I loved you, I still love you. You were and will be my only and my last love. It's not because you're broke that I'm not with you; it's because the loneliness and isolation of the country would be the death of me. You've never known anything else.

I am a miserable creature who despairs at your disdain. Forgive me, I beg you with hands clasped. I was maybe a little more to blame than I thought, but I won't dwell on it. Write me—but if it's like your last letter, then never write me again. I'll think of you as one thinks of God. I'll cherish your memory like I would that of an angel who held my hand. Believe me, if my body is impure, there is a place in it so pure where I will enclose your proposal. All

that I have is yours; do what you will with it. I'd like to give you a little of the good that I've received from you. I have to see you. It's impossible that you'd make a move so desperate. Answer me. I'm going crazy! I love you.
Céleste

As soon as you're unhappy, you seek the people who love you. I looked for a refuge from my despair. I went to Page's, and she told me her troubles. We wept together, because sadness was in her house too. She had lost her little Marie. I went back to my house and regrets: My first appearance in these rooms began with a fight that had nearly cost me my life. I felt like the place kept bringing bad luck.

To help me with my decision, here's how Robert responded:

I asked you to never write me again. Your letters make me ill, and I suffer enough without you igniting the debris of my existence.

All your words are lies. The place where your heart was, like your bedroom, is carried off by the highest bidder. I don't blush at my devotion to you. I regret nothing. You only had one thing to give me in exchange for my love, your empathy. You sold it—to this one for money, to that one for pleasure. I gave you my whole life, and you sullied it. You wanted to see if you could drive me to physical and moral ruin, with intent, tenacity, and premeditation, the way you do everything. You announced it to the world, and you kept your word. Be glad in your triumph. I'll no longer place myself on the rack to fight a lover that I no longer have the means to pay. I leave at ten o'clock for Algier. Your money will be sent along. Don't think of me

as one thinks of God; that's blasphemy. The lies have to stop here.
 Robert

As I read, I paid for all that he had done for me with an hour of pain. We were done, and for my part, I dreamed more of avenging myself than justifying myself.

I rebel here at the end, and I'm tired of this shitty treatment that I don't deserve. When I met you, and you whisked me off to the countryside to your house, I had a few debts. A small amount would have been enough to cover them; you could have given it to me without even noticing it was gone. However, you left me to find what I needed from another man. I gambled, and after paying my most urgent debts and buying a few dresses, we won a little back during the revolution, and a small sum of money remained to me. Today, you treat me like the lowliest creature on earth. Even when I wanted, later, to stave off misery in the future, would I be more guilty now than five years ago?

I'm returning your letter, which eases my heart. I cannot continue a correspondence that depresses me. I'm tired of crying. Never a kind word. Adieu. Examine your own past and see if it's fair to say such horrible things to me. Before meeting me, you'd already taken great strides toward losing all your money. Is it fair to hold me responsible for all your unhappiness? Adieu. I'll make sure you don't hear another word from me, but I'll never forget you.
 Céleste

www.ingramcontent.com/pod-product-compliance
Lightning Source LLC
Chambersburg PA
CBHW021146160426
43194CB00007B/705